I0084885

THE TALE OF TWO ADAMS

CHRIS CAUGHEY

MGK Press
Cedar Ridge, California

© 2002 by Chris Caughey

First published 2008

Published by MGK Press
taleoftwoadams@gmail.com and taleoftwoadams.blogspot.com

All rights reserved. No part of this publication may be reproduced, stored in a retrieval system, or transmitted in any form or by any means—for example, electronic, photocopy, recording—without the prior written permission of the publisher. The only exception is brief quotations in printed reviews.

ISBN 978-0-615-24140-1

LCCN 2008907318

Unless otherwise indicated, Scripture is the author's own translation of the original Hebrew and Greek.

Scripture quotations marked "NKJV™" are taken from the New King James Version®. Copyright © 1982 by Thomas Nelson, Inc. Used by permission. All rights reserved.

"Scripture quotations taken from the New American Standard Bible®, Copyright © 1960, 1962, 1963, 1968, 1971, 1972, 1973, 1975, 1977, 1995 by The Lockman Foundation. Used by permission." (www.Lockman.org)

"New Revised Standard Version Bible, copyright 1989, Division of Christian Education of the National Council of the Churches of Christ in the United States of America. Used by permission. All rights reserved."

Cover design: Rob Ryan

Contents

Acknowledgments

I NEED TO THANK my wife and children for all of their love, encouragement and constructive criticism as I wrote this book. They have been my biggest fans during this whole process. I could not have done it without them. I am deeply grateful to God for the privilege of learning everything about which I write in this book from Dr. Meredith G. Kline. He was my professor and my friend. If there is anything good or helpful in this book, the credit needs to go to that brilliant scholar who was more passionate about the Gospel than anyone else I know. My faith in, and devotion to the Lord, the Last Adam, was only profoundly deepened under his instruction. Very little (if anything) in this book is original. The reader should consider it largely a distillation of Dr. Kline's written corpus and lecture material from his *Pentateuch* and *Prophets* courses. The Lord called Dr. Kline home to the very upper-register which saturated everything he said, did and thought on April 13, 2007. I look forward to the day I will see Dr. Kline again in glory because of the accomplishment of our Savior. Thanks are also due to the Wilson family, especially Bob and Cameron. In many ways, this book would not have been written without their kind help. I must also thank Kevin Pischke, Rob Ryan and Dan Miller for their technical expertise. This book would likely have stalled out without them. Finally, I owe a debt of gratitude to Matt and Kim Gilliland of Woodglen Press for their patient help and advice.

Introduction

Introduction

"I am astonished that you are so quickly turning away from the one who called you in the grace of Christ to another gospel, which is not another Gospel—except that some are confusing you, and want to pervert the Gospel of Christ. But even if we, or an angel from Heaven should preach to you a gospel besides the one we preached to you, let him be damned. As we just told you, so now I say it again: if anyone preaches to you a gospel besides the one you received, let him be damned."
The Apostle Paul, Galatians 1:6-9

Those are strong words. The Apostle Paul was obviously concerned about the new Gentile Christians in Galatia who were being seduced by the Judaizers. The Judaizers were a group of Jews who taught that faith in Christ was indeed necessary for a person to be right with God... but so was keeping at least parts of the Law of Moses. They said, "If you are not circumcised according to the Law of Moses, you cannot be saved" (Acts 15:1). What we know about the Judaizers, we mostly infer from Paul's letters and the kinds of ideas he was arguing against. This much, at least, is clear: the Judaizers couldn't (or wouldn't) distinguish clearly between works and grace when it came to salvation.

Not much has changed. That is not because 21st century culture is so much like the culture of the 1st century. Culture, though good, is not where the "action" is, biblically speaking. Instead, the Bible is concerned about the history of the revelation of God's kingdom by means of covenants. In that case, not much has changed because since Adam broke the original covenant, sinners have always wanted to contribute some of their own work to their standing before God. That desire to contribute may be understandable (in light of the Fall), but Paul says that any teaching which promotes that contribution is damnable (in light of the Gospel of Jesus Christ).

Yet some people are still promoting a confusion of works and grace with respect to the Gospel. In light of what Paul said, I find it hard to believe that such people *intend* to blur the line between works and grace. After all, it seems to be *confusion* in thinking and reasoning that produces the muddling of works and grace. Nevertheless, such confusion is being taught to the Church at large by seminary professors who teach pastors who preach to their congregations. Other people are being confused by what they hear on the radio or read in popular books.

No matter where the confusion comes from, my purpose in this book is to show that covenant theology and the Gospel of salvation are inseparably joined together; however, if we misunderstand covenant theology—*and if we're consistent with our misunderstanding of covenant theology*—we will misunderstand the Gospel of salvation. Fortunately, however, though many teachers and authors misunderstand covenant theology, yet because they have not thought enough about the connection between covenant theology and the Gospel, they still proclaim the same Gospel that Paul so passionately defended and preached.

My labors in this book will be for the purpose of defending the Gospel that Paul preached, against other "gospels" that would compete with Paul's. I will do this in somewhat the same way that Paul did it in Galatians 3: by taking a look at the biblical covenants and their relationships to each other. We will begin with the first covenant that the Father made with creation and Adam, and we will conclude with the New Covenant that the Last Adam mediated between the Father and His covenant people. By studying justification via an examination of all of God's covenants from creation to consummation, from beginning to end, this book will also serve as an introduction to covenant theology. During our walk through the main story line of the Bible—the tale of two Adams—it should become clear that justification depends in various ways on *all* of God's covenants. But before we dive right in, some definitions are in order.

1

What Are You Talking About?

What Are You Talking About?

Definitions are always important when considering something as important as the Gospel of Jesus Christ. After all, if we make a mistake in defining a term that is basic and foundational to our investigation, our conclusion could turn out to be completely wrong.

It is something like using a map and a compass on a hike during a backpacking trip. Suppose you, an avid angler, want to navigate from your base camp to a remote lake, which is rumored to have superior fishing. If you don't correctly determine where your base camp is on the map, it is unlikely that your compass will help you find anything you're looking for. Of course, you could accidentally stumble onto the legendary lake. But in a backpacking situation, knowledge of where you are and where you are going could mean the difference between life and death.

In the same way, if we don't get our bearings—biblically speaking—in terms of concepts that are foundational to the Gospel, it is unlikely that our study will bring us to the Gospel of Jesus Christ. For if Jesus is the way, the truth and the life—if no one comes to the Father but through him—then any other so-called "gospel" is actually bad news, leaving us to die in our sins. So let's get back to basics.

COVENANT

Sometimes it seems as if there are as many different definitions of covenant as there are teachers. A seminary professor gives one definition, a popular radio teacher gives a different definition and a noted author gives yet another definition. Which one should we believe, and what difference does it make?

In developing a definition of biblical covenants, we should strive to be able to describe each and every covenant in Scripture. If our definition fails to account for just one of the biblical covenants (even if it does a good job of describing the rest of them) then it is not complete enough to be accurate.

For example, one author defines covenant as "a bond in blood sovereignly administered"[1] and "the result of a covenant commitment is the establishment of a relationship 'in connection with,' 'with' or 'between' people."[2] On the surface, that may appear to be a reasonable definition, able to account for all biblical covenants. But it has two main problems. First, consider the covenant which God announces and makes after Noah and his family safely exit the ark in Genesis 8:20-9:17. It is not a covenant between two parties of persons. It is not a covenant between God and all of humanity. It is not even a covenant between God and his own special people who are set apart from all other people. It is a covenant made between God and all of creation. The second problem with this definition is that it unnecessarily restricts covenants to bonds, which are unable to be broken or violated.[3] Thus, it has no place for covenants of works in which obedience earns the reward and disobedience earns the punishment. For now, we simply note that this definition cannot do justice to all of the biblical examples of covenants.

Another definition concludes, "a divine covenant is a sovereign administration of grace and promise."[4] In other words, *all* covenants are gracious. This may sound like a good definition. But like the previous definition, it is too narrow to include all of the biblical covenants. Covenants that operate according to a principle other than grace or promise simply do not exist, using this second

---

[1] O. Palmer Robertson, *The Christ of the Covenants* (Michigan: Baker Book House, 1980), 4.

[2] Ibid., 6.

[3] Ibid., 4.

[4] John Murray, *The Covenant of Grace* (Phillipsburg: P&R Publishing, 1953), 31.

definition. So, for example, when we come to the *covenant* (Deut. 5:2, 3; Lev. 26:14-20) that Israel entered into with God, we must try to reconcile *grace* with this:

> But if you will not obey me, and do not observe all these commandments, if you spurn my statutes, and abhor my ordinances, so that you will not observe all my commandments, and you break my covenant, I in turn will do this to you: I will bring terror on you; consumption and fever that waste the eyes and cause life to pine away. You shall sow your seed in vain, for your enemies shall eat it. I will set my face against you, and you shall be struck down by your enemies; your foes shall rule over you, and you shall flee though no one pursues you. And if in spite of this you will not obey me, I will continue to punish you seven fold for your sins. I will break your proud glory, and I will make your sky like iron and your earth like copper. Your strength shall be spent to no purpose: your land shall not yield its produce, and the trees of the land shall not yield their fruit. (Lev. 26:14-20, NRSV)

We will take a closer look at grace later in this chapter, but this obviously does not sound like the Gospel that Paul preached.

More importantly, however, this means that the covenant into which God created Adam, and the covenant which God the Father made with God the Son either cannot be considered in our study of covenant theology, or it means that both (pre-Fall) Adam and Christ needed the Father's *grace* and *promise* in order to keep their covenants. Neither option is helpful, and we will see why when we examine the relationship between grace and justice, faith and works.

This may all sound very technical and tedious—perhaps even unnecessary and unimportant. It is true that technical theological language can be very difficult for those who have not been formally trained in theology. But that doesn't make the technical language unimportant—just like a medical doctor's technical language (and scribbles on prescriptions), while difficult for those of us who have never been to medical school, is very important. Hopefully this book will highlight the importance of theological concepts while making those concepts easy to understand.

A third definition describes a *covenant* "as a divinely established relationship of union and communion between God and his people in the bonds of mutual love and faithfulness."[5] On the surface, this shares the same problem as the first definition above: it ignores the covenant that God made with *all of creation* in Genesis 8 and 9. It also shares some of the same problems as the second definition. However, this third definition has some unique elements that make a big difference.

Note that the third definition says covenant love and faithfulness are *mutual*. The word "mutual" means that in covenants where God is one party and man is the other party, *both* God *and* man must keep the covenant in terms of love for one another and faithfulness to one another. This definition also says that divine grace and human responsibility are not antithetical to each other. They are the two sides, or the two parts of the covenant that God has made with us and with our children.[6] The "doctrine of the covenant, [has] two parts, promise and obligation."[7] Therefore, on this third definition, all covenants operate according

---

[5] Shepherd, Norman. *The Call of Grace: How the Covenant Illuminates Salvation and Evangelism* (Phillipsburg: P&R Publishing, 2000), 12.

[6] Ibid., 9.

[7] Ibid., 63.

to divine grace or promise, and all covenants also operate according to human responsibility or obligation. At first glance, there may not seem to be a problem with seeing *grace* in all covenants, but the problem with seeing human responsibility or obligation (works) as an equal part with God's grace in all covenants ought to be immediately obvious.

Scripture tells us that in the history of God's covenantal dealings with man, something horrible happened. The first man and woman broke the covenant with God by being unfaithful. God told Adam and his wife not to eat of the tree of the knowledge of good and evil "for in the day that you eat from it you shall certainly die." (Gen. 2:17) In terms of what they were told *not* to do, covenant faithfulness for Adam and his wife meant abstaining from the tree of the knowledge of good and evil. But they ate the fruit and were unfaithful to God's covenant. The apostle Paul tells us in Romans 5:12, that Adam's covenant disobedience plunged all of humanity into a condition of sin and rebellion against God. The rest of Scripture testifies to this as well:

> "And the Lord saw that the evil of man was abundant on the earth, and the formation of every thought of his heart was evil continually." (Gen. 6:5)

> "...for the imagination of man's heart is evil from his youth..." (Gen. 8:21)

> "All of us, like sheep, have gone astray; each of us has turned to his own way..." (Is. 53:6)

> "We have all become like someone who is unclean; all of our righteousness is like [used] menstrual cloths..." (Is. 64:6)

> "The heart is more deceitful than all and incurably sick; who can know it?" (Jer. 17:9)

> "...for we have already made the indictment that all—both Jew and Greek—are under sin. Just as it is written, 'There is no one righteous, not even one. There is no one who understands; there is no one who seeks God. Everyone has turned away; together they are made worthless; there is no one who does good, not a single one.'" (Rom. 3:9-12)

> "For all have sinned, and have fallen short of the glory of God." (Rom. 3:23)

So part of the problem with the third definition of covenant—i.e., that all divine covenants involve divine grace and human responsibility—is that it either ignores the seriousness of the Fall and its effects upon all humanity, or it requires God to lower His standard of righteousness in order for Him to accept the fallen members of His covenant as His beloved people (or both). If the New Covenant, of which we are a part (Heb. 9:14, 15), is based upon God's grace toward us and our responsibility to obey God every bit as much as God's covenant with Adam was based upon God's grace and Adam's responsibility, then what real difference does the Fall make? It seems as though the implication of the third definition is that we have the *ability* to be just as faithfully obedient (responsible) to God's covenant as Adam did *before the Fall*. But that is not what Scripture teaches.

It is obvious that before the Fall, Adam had the ability to sin, because he proved it when he ate the forbidden fruit in Genesis 3. But it should also be obvious that before the Fall, Adam had the ability *not to sin* because God had declared all of His creation (including Adam) "very good" (Gen. 1:31). What about us? Are we just like Adam in our covenantal relationship with God: able to sin *and* able *not to sin*? Of course not. The Scriptures quoted above prove that because of the Fall, we are only able to be unfaithful, disobedient, irresponsible covenant breakers. The Lord Jesus

Himself, taught that we had lost our ability to be God-seeking covenant keepers when he said, "...no one is able to come to Me unless it [the ability] has been given to him by the Father" (Jn. 6:65). As fallen descendants of Adam, we simply cannot obey God (Rom. 8:7). So our covenantal relationship to God cannot be compared to Adam's covenantal relationship to God *before the Fall*... unless God lowered His standard of righteousness from absolutely perfect obedience down to something far less so that both sinless Adam before the Fall, and we—his wicked children after the Fall—could have an equal opportunity at keeping God's covenant.

If you were like me in high school and college, you appreciated those teachers and professors who graded the major exams on a curve. That way, you didn't have to worry so much about failing. If you knew the ability of your classmates well enough, you could do "C" work and still get an "A" if you did "just about as good as" the person who scored the highest. We naturally tend to think of our relationship to God this way because we are fallen descendants of Adam's. We think (and sometimes we are even taught) that if we do good things outwardly—like having daily quiet times, witnessing to unbelievers, helping others, attending Sunday worship weekly, tithing regularly—we keep God's covenant "just about as good as" what God demands of His creatures, and thereby please Him. But again, this is plainly not what the Bible tells us. God demands: "Be holy, because I am holy" (1 Pet. 1:16; cf. Lev. 11:44). Jesus Himself said, "Therefore, you must be perfect as your heavenly Father is perfect" (Mt. 5:48; cf. Dt. 18:13). Note well: Jesus did not encourage us to do our best. God doesn't grade on a curve, He grades against the standard of His own perfection.

This highlights another problem with the third definition of a covenant. Even though we are sinful, and therefore unable to keep the perfectly righteous requirements which God demanded of Adam, the third definition still insists that in order for a covenant to be a covenant, God's people have obligations which must be met: faithfulness and responsibility. In other words, in every covenant,

God's people are obligated to keep the covenant in terms of their own personal faithfulness and responsibility. Sadly, this definition of a covenant eliminates the roles of Adam and Christ as the two great covenant representatives. Paul expounds upon this in two chapters of two of his epistles: Romans 5:12-19 and 1 Corinthians 15:40-50. Consider the following outline of Romans 5:

Romans 5	Adam	Christ
Verse 12	sin, death	
Verse 15	violation, death	free gift, grace
Verse 16	sin, judgment, punishment, condmenation, violations	gift, free gift, justification
Verse 17	violation, death	abundance of grace, gift of righteousness, reign in life
Verse 18	violation, condemnation	one act of righteousness, justification of life
Verse 19	disobedience, sinners	obedience, righteous

1 Corinthians 15 is similar:

1 Corinthians	Adam	Christ
Verse 40	terrestrial	celestial
Verse 42	perishable	imperishable
Verse 43	common/dishonor, weakness	glory, power
Verse 44	natural	Spiritual
Verse 45	first man Adam, living soul	Last Adam, life-giving Spirit
Verse 46	natural	Spiritual
Verse 47	first man, earth, earthy	second man, heavenly
Verse 48	earthy	heavenly
Verse 49	image of the earthly	image of the heavenly
Verse 50	flesh and blood, perishable	Kingdom of God, imperishable

Look back over the lists. There is no middle ground. You are either justified or condemned; you either have life or death. And yet, your place in either column is not determined by your actions. Your place—whether justified or condemned—is **determined by the actions of your representative**. All of humanity shares Adam as our first representative. It is because of Adam's Fall that we sin and die (Rom. 5:12). Adam's guilt is *imputed* or *credited* to our individual accounts so that we are considered by God as having sinned with Adam (Rom. 5:12-18[8]). Therefore, because of

---

[8] For perhaps the best treatment of this in print, see John Murray's short book, *The Imputation of Adam's Sin* (Phillipsburg: P&R Publishing, 1959). It is true that earlier, we took issue with his definition of covenant. But this is where we are thankful that Murray was inconsistent with his covenant theology, because his

the first Adam's Fall, we need the Last Adam (1 Cor. 15:45) as our obedient representative in order to be saved. Just as Adam's guilt is imputed to our individual accounts, so Christ's righteousness—His active law-keeping—is imputed to us so that we are considered by God as having obeyed Him and kept His covenant perfectly (Rom. 3:21, 22, 27, 28; 4:3-5, 22-24; 5:12-19; Phil. 3:9; 2 Cor. 5:21). God does not prescribe "Do-It-Yourself," self-help religion for His people, because He has ordained representatives to keep or break His covenant on behalf of His people.

If we define covenant in such a way as to make Adam, Christ, you and I all basically equals in the pursuit of God's favor and blessing, then we end up reasoning in much the same way as a fourth-century monk named Pelagius. Pelagius taught that Adam's descendants do not need God's grace in order to be saved because Adam's sin affected only himself. So human beings are not sinful, but neutral or even basically good. Therefore, reasoned Pelagius, Adam was merely a bad example, and Christ was merely a good example. We can obey God sufficiently on our own if we simply choose not to follow Adam's bad example, but choose instead to do what Jesus would do. For this, multiple Church councils rightly condemned Pelagius as a heretic. Of course, Pelagius was wrong. We are not covenantally related to God in the same way that Adam was before the Fall, and we certainly aren't covenantally related to God in the same way that Christ was as the sinless God-man (though some would say that Christ shares our same faith![9]).

But it is not enough to simply critique deficient definitions of a covenant. We must search the Scriptures to arrive at a

---

book on the imputation of Adam's sin defends the very foundations of the Gospel.

[9] Ibid., 19. Shepherd says, "All of this is made possible through the covenantal righteousness of Jesus Christ. His was a living, active and obedient faith that took him all the way to the cross. This faith was credited to him as righteousness."

sufficient definition—a definition of covenant that will be basic enough to describe *every* covenant in which God is one party. So we will begin by noting that a covenant is a certain kind of *relationship*. It is a particular way in which God *relates* to humanity and to the rest of His creation. That means that God relates to everything—creation, believers and unbelievers—by covenants. Since God is just and fair, covenants are *legal* relationships that God makes binding upon Himself and the other party in the particular covenants. That means that it would be unjust and unfair for either God or the other party to break the covenant as He has defined it. This is why the Bible only records two ways of treating a covenant: keeping it (Gen. 17:9, 10) or breaking it (Gen. 17:14); remembering it (Gen. 9:15, 16) or forgetting it (Dt. 4:23, 31). Finally, covenants involve the *swearing of an oath*, binding oneself to keep the terms of the covenant on pain of God's punishment or curse (Num. 30:2, 3, 13, 14; Ezek. 20:37; Jer. 27:2; Dan. 6:8).

The oath is important for more than one reason. First, it alerts us to what kind of covenant we are reading about based upon which party swears the oath. After the Fall, it becomes especially clear that if God swears the oath, we can be sure that it is a covenant governed by the principle of grace because God cannot lie (Heb. 6:18, Titus 1:2), He does not change (Mal. 3:6; Heb. 13:8), nor does He turn away from His intended course of action (James 1:17). If God says that He will keep the terms of a covenant, He will keep them regardless of anyone or anything else. On the other hand, if man swears the oath, we can be sure that it is a covenant that is governed by the principle of works or justice because man can change; he can lie; he can rebel. What is impossible for God (changing, lying, unfaithfulness) is quite possible for man. Second, oaths are important because they are so essential to covenants that even when the word "covenant" does not appear in the biblical text, if we read about an *oath*, we can be sure that we are reading about a covenant.

But what if someone breaks the covenant oath that he *personally* swore? There are *sanctions*—also known as consequences or future outcomes—attached to the covenant. There are blessing sanctions for *keeping* the covenant oath and there are curse sanctions for *violating* the covenant oath. Another way of talking about sanctions is to say that God *enforces* the covenants that He makes. After all, there is no one higher or more powerful than God to administer rewards and punishments fairly. Like oaths, the sanctions or consequences are so basic and essential to covenants that when we read about threats (curse sanctions) or offers (blessing sanctions) in Scripture, we know that we are reading about a covenant.

If we bring all these distinct elements together, we could say that a covenant (in which God is one party) is an *oath-sworn, legally binding relationship, enforced by God.* This definition is broad enough to be able to include every biblical instance of a covenant. You can pull out your Bible and test this. Find the word "covenant" or "oath" and see if our definition does not provide perfectly for what you read about in the Scriptures. However, arriving at a good definition of covenant is only the beginning. There are still many unanswered questions.

ESCHATOLOGY & THE ULTIMATE KINGDOM OF GOD: THE TIES THAT BIND

What do each of the biblical covenants have to do with each other? What do you and I have to do with all of these covenants? Is there anything that unites all of the different covenants together? Some would say that each covenantal period in history is distinct from all others because each historical period has a unique ruling factor—a particular way of God's administering His rule.[10] These

---

[10] Showers, Renald E., *There Really Is A Difference!: A Comparison of Covenant and Dispensational Theology,* (Bellmawr: The Friends of Israel Gospel Ministry, Inc., 1990), 30. I readily acknowledge that not every Dispensationalist will agree with

people call themselves Dispensationalists and they certainly do not want to see the kind of unity of the covenants that we will see shortly. Others would say that all of the biblical covenants after the Fall are united to each other in terms of *continuity* rather than separated or distinguished in terms of *discontinuity*. Most popular covenant theologians would identify with this second category. Historically, covenant theologians have recognized both legitimate continuities and discontinuities between the various covenants.

However, the Bible also seems to unite the covenants in terms of eschatology and the Kingdom of God (the *reign* of God and the *realm* from which He reigns). Eschatology? Many of us associate eschatology with the "end times," millennial positions or maybe even theories of tribulation and the rapture. Why bring it up now? Have we reached the end of the book already? Hardly. Instead of imprisoning it at the *end* of the book, we need to re-orient ourselves to eschatology as it is revealed to us on the pages of Holy Scripture. It is not merely about "what happens at the end," but it is also about why there is a beginning and where everything is headed. Dr. Lane Tipton offers four helpful ways of thinking about eschatology that we would do well to consider. Biblical eschatology is:

1) The *eternal reality of the Kingdom Paradise* which God promised to Adam in the Covenant of Works.

2) The *immutable* or *unchangeable state of perfect life in the presence of God*.

3) The *heavenly goal of the promised Kingdom* under the Covenant of Works.

---

such a short summary of Dispensationalism. Certainly there are more features and nuances than time and space permit us to explore. My goal here is simply to allow a Dispensationalist to succinctly articulate his view in his own words.

4) The *final stage of the Kingdom of God.*[11]

You can see that this orientation views eschatology as present and active even from the very *beginning* of the Bible. It is not merely the tail that is pinned on the end of redemption—it is the pattern for creation. It does not merely look forward to the end times—it also looks up to the heavenly reality that God created in order to dwell with His human creatures forever. Though we will look more closely at the biblical evidence for this in the next chapter, it will suffice for now to say that Adam was offered the ultimate goal of the heavenly kingdom of God. That is part of the reason that Paul can compare and contrast Adam and Christ the way he does in Romans 5:12-18, 1 Corinthians 15:40-50 and Ephesians 5:22-33.[12] So if Adam represented all of humanity as he attempted to earn the right for us to enter the eternal kingdom of heaven, and if Christ accomplished what Adam failed to do—as those passages teach—then the only distinction between groups of people and their eternal destinies is the distinction between the people of God destined for eternal life in the final kingdom of God on the one hand, and those who are not the people of God, destined for eternal death in hell on the other hand. God's ultimate goal for humanity proves the unified purpose for all of the biblical covenants in terms of works (Adam, Moses, Christ) and grace (Gen. 3:15, Gen. 8:22-ch. 9, Abraham, the New Covenant). The legitimate continuity between and organizing principle for all the covenants—pre-redemptive (before the Fall) and redemptive (after the Fall)—is God's sovereign purpose to secure a people for

---

[11] This was taken from a lecture Dr. Tipton gave on the Covenant of Works at Grace Orthodox Presbyterian Church. An audio version of the lecture is available at www.two-age.org/online_sermons.htm#LTipton. See "1. Eschatological Focus (Vos)," or contact the tape ministry at Grace Orthodox Presbyterian Church at: 1419 Beaver Rd., Osbourne, PA 15143; (412) 741-3430.

[12] In Ephesians 5:22-33, notice that Paul quotes Genesis 2:24 where God has just created the woman out of Adam's rib. In this way, Paul compares Christ with Adam, and he compares the Church with Eve.

Himself in order to dwell with them eternally in His heavenly kingdom. God uses the covenants in order to exercise His kingship and administer His kingdom both in its earthly representations and its ultimate form.

JUSTICE AND WORKS: THE PERFECTLY FAIR REQUIREMENTS OF GOD

It goes without saying that *God is just.* Not only do Christians know that because God tells us as much in the Bible (Gen. 18:25; Dt. 32:4; Job 8:3), but even non-Christians know that God is just. That is why non-Christian religions feel the need to appease angry and offended gods. That is why psychologists and psychiatrists have more business than they can handle. As covenant creatures who are fallen because of the sin of our covenant representative, Adam, we know deep down in the cores of our beings that God demands perfect obedience from us (Mat. 5:48), and that because of Adam, we have failed to give Him what He demands.

We must keep in mind not only that God is just, but what justice is. The principle of justice is simple: you get what you *deserve.* A simple illustration can demonstrate this. Suppose Cameron is of driving age. He would really like to drive his father's restored 1949 Chevy truck. However, Cameron's father, Bob, has told him that if he drives it, he will lose every privilege he has until his eighteenth birthday. At the same time, if Cameron does not drive the truck, Bob will buy Cameron the brand new Ferrari sports car he has been wanting at the next holiday to come along.

It might be helpful to think of the rewards and punishments in terms of cause and effect. The loss of privileges or the Ferrari do not just "drop out of the sky" for no reason at all. Each possible consequence depends upon how Cameron responds to his father's rule about not driving the truck. Cameron's *works* are the cause, and the consequences (the loss of privileges *or* the Ferrari) are the *effects*. So Cameron's *response* to the rule becomes the *cause* of his receiving one of the consequences; and when he receives one of the consequences, that *consequence* is the *effect* of his response to the rule. Cameron's obedience will cause the effect of his receiving a brand new Ferrari sports car. But Cameron's disobedience will cause the effect of the loss of every privilege he has.

We might ask ourselves what kind of cause this story illustrates. The answer is that it is a *meritorious* cause. "Merit" is not a bad word, and it should not cause us to recoil in shock, horror or disgust. Merit simply means value or worth; it refers to what something deserves. Cameron's father had attached positive value and worth to Cameron's obedience and negative value and worth to Cameron's disobedience. Bob had announced that Cameron's obedience *deserved* a new Ferrari and that Cameron's disobedience *deserved* the loss of all privileges. That does not make Bob any less of a father, and it does not in any way contradict or lessen Bob's fatherly love for Cameron.

The same is true of the relationship between our Heavenly Father and us. **God is just.** That means that He rewards actions according to what *He says* they deserve (Job 34:11; Is 59:18; Jer. 17:10; Ezek. 18:4; 1 Cor. 3:8). Yet this does not mean that He does not love us as creatures uniquely created in His image. It simply means that as the sovereign Lord, He reserves the right to attach value and worth to our obedience and disobedience; He reserves the right to tell us what our actions deserve or merit.

Some would say that this casts a shadow on God and somehow diminishes his capacity as our Heavenly Father by turning him into our employer.[13] While such a view seems to want to

---

[13] Shepherd, Norman. *The Call of Grace.* (Phillipsburg: P&R, 2000), 60. "On a deeper level, what must be challenged...is the very idea of merit itself." Cf. "First, if we do not reject the idea of merit, we are not really able to challenge the

preserve God's sovereignty and love by rejecting the possibility of meriting Heaven, what it doesn't seem to recognize as the logical conclusion of a rejection of merit *in principle* (or by definition), is that if it were impossible for Adam to deserve eternal life in Heaven by his obedience, *then it would be equally impossible for Adam to deserve eternal death in Hell for his disobedience.* If he cannot merit the reward, then he cannot merit the punishment either. The other problem that a categorical rejection of merit causes is that if God still gives out rewards and punishments, He does not do it on the basis of justice or fairness—so that someone could be perfectly faithful to God yet still receive eternal death in Hell because his or her faithfulness is not meritorious (i.e., of value, worthy, deserving) and God simply picked a consequence randomly out of His hat. But, of course, Adam did deserve Hell, because that is what God said Adam's disobedience deserved (Gen. 2:17); and not only did Adam deserve Hell, but we also deserve Hell because he acted as our covenant representative (Rom. 5:12-18).

So a denial of any kind of human merit actually undermines and removes the very foundations of the Gospel by detaching and divorcing human actions from their God-decreed consequences. In other words, the Gospel *depends upon* human merit. Think about it. If human responses to God's covenant demands do not have value, worth or merit, then it would have been impossible not only for Adam to earn Heaven for us (1 Cor. 15:45), but it would have been equally impossible for him to earn Hell for us (Rom. 5:12). By the same token, Christ would have been unable to earn the Kingdom of Heaven for us (John 17:4, 5; Eph. 1:10c, 11), and it would have been meaningless for Him to have been punished for the valueless, worthless, merit-less actions of other.

Romanist doctrine of salvation at its very root." (pp. 61, 62) "God does not, and never did, relate to his people on the basis of a works/merit principle." (p. 60)

It would be a matter of our mere speculation about God to say that covenants of justice or works are an unloving or unkind way for God to relate to anyone. But it is a matter of God's own revelation to us (both general and special) that He has in fact covenantally related to human beings in terms of justice. By way of general principle, the apostle Paul says "to the one who works, his wages are not accounted according to a free favor, but according to what is owed to him by obligation" (Rom. 4:4). In other words, if someone is related to God based on works, then that person gets what that person deserves. Paul says plainly that the wages (i.e. "what that person deserves") are owed to him by obligation. In covenants of works, God has *obligated* Himself to reward good works and punish evil works according to the way He arranged the covenant. He *owes* the person either a blessing or a curse for the work that he or she did.

In the specific case of Genesis 2, verses 16 and 17, God tells us that Adam would deserve or earn eternal death in Hell *if* he ate the fruit of the Tree of the Knowledge of Good and Evil (in the next chapter, we will examine the evidence for God's offer to Adam of the ultimate kingdom *if* he obeyed). In Leviticus 26, God tells us that Israel would deserve or earn many material blessings *if* they kept the Mosaic Law. In the same chapter, He tells us that Israel would deserve or earn many material curses *if* they broke or violated the Mosaic Law. In John 17, verses 4 and 5, our Lord Jesus acknowledges not only that His Father gave Him work to do, but that because He has finished that work He *deserves* glorification.

These specific instances of covenants based upon God's justice and human works—especially the covenant of creation—provide the foundation or the skeleton for the covenants based upon God's free grace. The reason for this is simple: God did not stop being God even when Adam fell. He did not even stop being God when He began to covenantally relate to His people on the basis of free grace. **God was still just.** Thus, if God told Adam that Heaven must be earned by his obedience, then even after the Fall,

Heaven must still be earned by *Someone's* obedience even if fallen man could not earn it himself. If Heaven did not have to be earned after the Fall, then God would have changed—something He Himself tells us He cannot do, for if He could, the future would be absolutely uncertain (Mal. 3:6). In the same way, if God told Adam that he would certainly die if he disobeyed, then even after the Fall, *Someone* would have to pay that ultimate death penalty even if fallen man could not do it himself. If no one died under God's ultimate curse, His perfectly just and fair threat would be meaningless and harmless. God's justice was not changed by the Fall. In order for *anyone* to enjoy eternal life in the ultimate kingdom of God, *Someone* whose obedience to God's law was worthy or meritorious enough would have to be punished by God for the sins of others; *Someone* whose righteousness was worthy or meritorious enough would have to meet God's standard of obedience on behalf of others.

GRACE: THE REMEDY FOR SIN

While everybody knows that God is just because we have His law written on our hearts as His creatures who bear His image (Rom. 2:14, 15), we only know about God's grace because "the Word became flesh and tabernacled among us" (John 1:14, 17, 18; Rom. 3:21-24) and the fact that God's Word (the Bible) is entirely about that Word which became flesh (Luke 24:25-27, 44-45; John 5:39, 46-47; 1 Pet. 1:10-11). But as with "covenant" and "justice," we must also define "grace" biblically if we are going to follow God's reasoning all the way to the gospel that Paul preached. As odd as it may seem at first, the biblical definition of grace depends not only upon the biblical definition of justice, but it also assumes that God's justice has already been violated. If justice is getting what you deserve, then grace is getting the blessing that you *don't* deserve *in spite of* your sin. Probably the most popular definition of grace used by most seminary professors, Bible teachers and ministers is "unmerited favor." But "unmerited" and the idea of "God's niceness" just don't go far enough. Let's return to our illustration.

Suppose Cameron decides that he is going to drive his father's 1949 Chevy truck even though his father has warned him of the consequences. Perhaps he plans to bring it back and park it in exactly the same spot which Bob had parked it, hoping that nobody would notice that it had been driven. Unfortunately, while on his joy ride, Cameron collides with an empty bus, totaling the truck.

Justice demands that Bob strip Cameron of all privileges, because that is what he told Cameron would happen if he drove the truck (not to mention *damaged* the truck!). However, if—in spite of Cameron's flagrant disobedience and destruction of his father's property—Bob took upon *himself* the loss of privileges, paid for the police citation, the damage to the bus and his truck *and* bought Cameron the brand new Ferrari sports car anyway, *that* would be grace.

You see, while justice requires merit, grace requires *demerit*. Bob's purchase of the Ferrari for Cameron was not Bob's *unmerited* favor. If, all things being equal, Bob had simply bought Cameron the Ferrari—without any reference to the 1949 Chevy truck, without reference to anything—if he had bought Cameron the Ferrari for no apparent reason at all, *that* would be *unmerited* favor. It would be a kind favor on Bob's part, but Cameron would not have done anything to *deserve* the gift. But by driving and wrecking his father's truck in direct violation of his father's command, Cameron's actions were the opposite of meritorious; they were *demeritorious*. **Cameron's actions *deserve* punishment.** And yet, that is the only context in which there can be grace.

If this sounds like the Gospel message, it should. God's grace to us is not unmerited—He did not simply give us eternal life for no apparent reason. He gave us eternal life in spite of the fact that our sin is as offensive to Him as if we had just mugged Him in the back alley, beaten Him, raped Him and left Him for dead. Adam knew what God required: "...from the tree of the knowledge of good and evil you shall not eat, for in the day you eat of it, you will certainly die" (Gen. 2:17). But he ate of the forbidden tree anyway. God's justice demanded that Adam and his wife (and all of subsequent humanity whom Adam represented) experience the ultimate death that God had threatened, for Adam's actions were not meritorious but *demeritorious*. Adam's disobedience *deserved* eternal death in Hell. Yet in *spite* of what Adam deserved, God promised that from Eve would come One who would not only receive the curse or punishment which Adam deserved, but would achieve the victory which Adam was to have earned. The favor that God showed to Adam and Eve (and to all His people) was demerited. Yet His favor did not contradict His justice, because Christ would bear the punishment that Adam and we deserved, as well as earn the reward that Adam was supposed to have earned.

You can see that the ultimate reward is never received by a combination of grace and justice. It is either one or the other. For example, Adam was to receive the Kingdom by his works according to God's justice. We will receive the Kingdom by faith in Christ according to God's grace. Far from being two equal tools to be used in attaining salvation, works and grace are opposed to each other when it comes to how we receive the inheritance of the Kingdom of God. Paul says this explicitly more than once. In Romans 11:6, he says: "But if it is by grace, it is no longer on the basis of works; otherwise, grace is no longer grace" (NASB). In the same way, he says, "For if the inheritance is based upon the Law, it is no longer based upon the Promise; but God gave it to Abraham by the Promise" (Gal. 3:18). The presence of one (works or grace) excludes the possibility of the other.

With regard to the principle of justice, the cause and effect relationship between works and sanctions was that the works were the cause and the sanctions (reward for obedience, punishment for disobedience) were the effects (Rom. 4:4). Adam was to obey God perfectly, and God would justly reward him with eternal life in the New Heavens and New Earth. However, in the case of grace, the cause and effect relationship between works and sanctions is completely reversed. With grace, the reward or blessing is the *cause* and our good works are the *effect*. If Romans 4:4 described the principle of justice and works, then Romans 4:5 describes the principle of grace and faith. Paul says,

> To the one who works, his wages are not accounted according to grace, but according to what is owed to him by obligation. But to the one who does not work, but trusts Him who justifies the *wicked*, his faith is imputed to him as righteousness (Rom. 4:4-5, emphasis mine).

In verse 4, God *owes* a blessing or a curse to the person who works. But in verse 5, notice the person whom God justifies: it is not *merely* the person who does not work. In verse 5, God justifies the *wicked*. Here we see that according to the principle of grace, God blesses the person who deserves punishment because of his wickedness—His blessing or favor is *demerited*. Even though we deserve eternal punishment because we are wicked, God sent His only-begotten Son to become one of us in order to earn for us the rewards of forgiveness of sin, righteousness, holiness and the perfection of the New Creation—and *because* of what Christ earned, we do good works.

Of course, this is because of eschatology. Adam's goal (eschatology) as a creature of *this* creation, was eternal life in the New Creation. Yet Adam didn't *need* that New Life in order to obey God because there was nothing bad about *any* aspect of creation. God created Adam with everything he needed in order to do what God required of him. Adam's obedience would be the cause, and the New Creation would be the effect. After the Fall, however, the story is completely different. As a result of the Fall, human beings are characterized by death and sin (Rom. 5:12; Gen. 3:19; 1 Cor. 15:21, 22). Adam's Fall produced in every facet of human beings, a wicked corruption (Rom. 3:10-18; Ps. 51:5; Jer. 17:9) so severe that the apostle Paul says that "...there is *none who seeks God*; all have turned away, they have together become depraved" (Rom. 3:11, 12 emphasis mine). Thus, Adam and we, his fallen children, *cannot* obey God for the simple reason that sinners (left to themselves) do what comes naturally: they sin (disobey). That is why Paul said, "For the mind of the flesh is an enemy of God's; it does not obey the Law of God, nor is it able to [obey]" (Rom. 8:7).

That is what our life is like as fallen descendants of Adam's. Unlike Adam *before* the Fall, we do need the new Life of the New Creation in order to obey God. But as depraved people, we have no way of obtaining that New Life for ourselves. It is still the goal for us, as it was for Adam. But now, because of Christ's meritorious obedience, substitutionary death, victorious resurrection and royal ascension, He has earned that New Life for us so that we have the ability to obey God. Whereas for Adam, his obedience was the cause and the New Creation was the effect—for us, being New creatures in Christ Jesus (2 Cor. 5:17) is the cause and our obedience is the effect (Eph. 2:10).

While it is true that the New Creation did not begin to dawn upon the scene of history until Christ's resurrection, this reversal of the cause and effect relationship has been true for all of God's people since the Fall. After all, the author of Hebrews says that the people of God *immediately* after the Fall—Abel, Enoch, Noah, Abraham, Isaac, Jacob, Sara and many more—had the substance or essence of "the things which are being hoped for" (Heb. 11:1) by faith. In other words, by *faith*, they were all—like us— "looking for that city which has foundations, whose builder and craftsman is God" (Heb. 11:10; Titus 3:7). In the Bible, faith always accompanies grace (Eph. 2:8, 9; Gal. 3:11, 14; Rom. 1:5; 3:24, 27; 4:16; 5:2) and works always accompany justice or Law (Gal. 2:16; 3:2, 5, 12; Rom. 3:28; Rom. 4:4). So *all* of God's children after the Fall have eternal life only by God's grace through faith in Christ.

That is why we can speak of the Covenant of Grace that has been in force since the Fall, and will be in force until Christ returns to judge the living and the dead. However, some people don't think we have the right to speak of "the Covenant of Grace." "Where is that term or phrase in Scripture?" they ask. Yet there are many terms and phrases we use that are absolutely true, even though they don't appear anywhere within the pages of the Bible. For example, you won't find the term "Trinity" anywhere in Scripture, yet it teaches the foundational truth that God is one in essence and three in person with crystal clarity. The "imputed righteousness of Christ" as an exact phrase is absent from the pages of the Bible, yet there is no hope of standing before God without it. You will search your Bible in vain to find the word "inerrancy," yet there is no point in taking the Bible seriously without it. In the same way, we don't find the exact phrase, "the Covenant of Grace" in the Bible, yet the Bible clearly teaches that any fallen human being who will have eternal life, will have it by grace alone, through faith alone because of Christ alone.

JUSTIFICATION: GOD'S FAVORABLE VERDICT

Now we will see the doctrinal "strands" of justification, covenant, eschatology or the ultimate kingdom of God, works and grace woven into one secure chord of salvation. First, not only does God administer or rule his kingdom by using covenants, but justification is the desired outcome of the covenants that look forward to that kingdom—covenants like the eternal covenant between the Father and the Son, the Adamic covenant, the Abrahamic covenant and the New covenant. Second, justification is eschatological. In other words, justification always has a view to the ultimate Kingdom of God, because being declared righteous in God's sight (justification) is the condition that must be met in order to enter that kingdom. Finally, justification is based upon the good works of the covenant representatives and it is based upon grace for the members of the covenant of grace.

That is why we Protestants have (historically) been so jealous to safeguard the doctrine of justification as the heart of the gospel.

Contrary to official Roman Catholic opinion, Reformers like Martin Luther[14] and John Calvin were not malcontents who just couldn't get along with the Church-at-large. They were men who were passionately committed to the Gospel of Jesus Christ, and were willing to part ways with any who promoted "another" gospel. I often wonder how many in the Church today are willing to do the same.

Of course, how we define justification is as critical now, as it was back in the sixteenth century. But most Christians today seem to wonder what all the fuss was about. In fact, you might ask, "How relevant to my life, is the doctrine of justification? After all, I live in the real world, and I don't have much to do with lofty, ivory-tower theology." Yet if you stop to think for a moment, you'll see that you think about justification more than you realize. Have you ever felt as though some bad thing that happened to you was the result of God being angry with you for something that you had done (or left undone)? After doing something good, have you ever secretly felt as though God was more pleased with you than He was before? Or have you ever felt as though something good that happened to you (getting a lot of money, having valuable objects) was God's blessing for some obedient thing you had done for him? If you answered "yes" to any or all of those questions, you have thought about justification—even if you didn't think about the *word* "justification."

You see, justification has to do with how we are right with God. So what we believe about justification is completely relevant for our everyday lives because it affects how we think, feel and live.

---

[14] Though Luther rightly understood that Christ provided for us the very righteousness that God demands of us, he did not seem to understand the relationships between covenant, eschatology and justification. We rejoice that he articulated the doctrine of justification as clearly as he did, because he did the Church a great service. But we call our Lutheran brethren to embrace a full-orbed and enriched doctrine of justification that includes the concepts of covenant and eschatology.

Growing up in broad evangelicalism[15], I could count on hearing something like this at every youth retreat: "Now some of you need to get right with God..." It was as if we *had been* right we God at one time, but now we weren't. Usually, the cure was said to be getting back into a daily ritual called a "quiet time" (i.e., private prayer and devotional Bible reading). But that was all very unnerving for me and for my sensitive conscience. I wondered, "What if the very next thing I do makes me *not* right with God again?" Consequently, I lived a pretty miserable life of guilt and shame. Of course, I had been programmed to say that I was saved by God's grace and not at all by my own works. I thought I believed that. But when the youth pastor said it was time to "get right with God," I also thought that I was right with God based upon what *I* did—*my* good works—*my* obedience (which, sadly, meant that I was pompous and self-righteous).

I wasn't alone in thinking that way. But some of my friends didn't share my sensitive conscience. They quickly grew tired of Christianity as we knew it because they realized that no matter how hard they tried, they were never right with God. Rather than living between guilt and shame on the one hand and arrogance and self-righteousness on the other, they decided that God's rules were for the birds. One thing was clear: none of us understood justification.

---

[15] By "broad evangelicalism," I mean that portion of the modern Church that still believes in the existence of the Triune, supernatural God and some Protestant fundamentals (e.g., the inerrancy of Scripture, the virgin birth and bodily resurrection of Christ, that Christ is the only savior, etc.). However, broad evangelicalism also tends to believe that doctrine is divisive, and so Sunday morning messages and praise choruses tend to marginalize the core tenets of the faith by focusing on private, personal experience, as well as what the latest polls reveal is "practical" (i.e., a felt need). Broad evangelicalism values orthopathos (right feeling) over orthodoxy (right belief), sentimentalism over gratitude, pietism over Word and sacrament piety, personal preferences or "rights" over wisdom, novelty over tradition, things private over things corporate and things subjective over things objective.

How do you think that you are right with God? In other words, how would you define justification? Perhaps the most popular definition is, "Justified: *just-as-if-I'd* never sinned." But that definition doesn't go far enough. It assumes that all God asks of us is that we merely be free of sin.[16] If we think of these definitions in terms of balancing our checkbook, it might look something like this:

	Debit or Demerit	Balance
	nothing	nothing
Total:		sinless

Or it may look something like this:

	Debit or Demerit	Balance
	SIN	SIN
Total:		sinful

There is a category of debit (demerit or sin) and of the balance (God's view of us). We can either have lots of debt and be sinful in

---

[16] For example, on page 19 of his unpublished paper "The Grace of Justification, February 8, 1979," (Westminster Theological Seminary in Philadelphia, photocopy), Norman Shepherd defines justification in completely negative terms of avoiding God's condemnation: "To escape the wrath and curse of God is to be no longer under condemnation, but to be forgiven and accepted by God. It is to be justified. In justification the obedience and satisfaction of Christ are imputed to believers so that they are no longer under the wrath and condemnation of God. Justification includes forgiveness (Rom. 4:7) and the one who is justified has peace, for the wrath and curse of God no longer threaten him (Rom. 5:1)."

God's estimation, or we can have no debt and be without sin in God's estimation.

But something is missing. Deep down, in places we don't talk about, we know that God demands more of us than merely avoiding sin or being forgiven for it. We know this, because God has written His righteous requirements on our hearts as His creatures that are uniquely made in His image (Rom. 2:14, 15). God demands that we keep his righteous requirements with absolute perfection (Mat. 5:48). Therefore, there is a third category in our justification "checkbook":

	Debit or Demerit	Credit or Merit	Balance
Total:			

So even if we leave merit or positive righteousness out of our definition of justification, we still have the gnawing sense that God demands it of us. But when we don't make room for the category of active righteousness that is measured by God's commands, then legalism and moralism automatically and unavoidably rush in to fill up that empty space in our definition. Legalism implicitly and subtly denies that Christ's work is enough, by requiring that we do something personally and individually to please God. Moralism is bare, abstract ethical prescriptions without any explicit consideration or understanding about what Christ has done for us.[17] We don't have to consciously try to introduce legalism or

---

[17] This is not to say that there is no place for ethics or morality in the Christian life. There certainly is a place for such things. However, ethics and morality must always be viewed through the lens of who Christ is, and what Christ has done for

moralism into our thinking. They are the "natural" way we sinners respond to the offended Creator.

Now when we factor in Romans 5:12-19 and the only two possible covenant representatives we can have, there are only two ways we can appear before God:

Figure 1

	Debit or Demerit	Credit or Merit	Balance
	sin x 9,999,999	nothing	sin x 9,999,999
Total:			unjust or condemned

Figure 2

	Debit or Demerit	Credit or Merit	Balance
	nothing	righteousness x 9,999,999	righteousness x 9,999,999
Total:			righteous or justified

---

us. Without constantly keeping Him as our representative in mind, ethics and morality rapidly degenerate into legalism and moralism. For example: Because God first loved us, we ought to love (1 Jn. 4:10, 19); because God has forgiven us for our offenses against Himself and others, we ought to forgive those who have offended us (Mt. 18:21-35); because we have been united with Christ in His death, we should not live as slaves to sin (Rom. 6:1-14).

Obviously, Figure 1 describes our situation. But we didn't come to be in this situation as individuals who just happen to all be sinful. Romans 5:12-14 teaches us that we are sinful because Adam who represented us, broke God's covenant. As our legal representative before the Almighty Judge, his actions were counted by God as if they were our actions. The word that the Bible uses to describe this transaction is *imputed*. To impute something means to "reckon," "account" or "credit" something to someone's account in a way that is legally binding. Even though you and I did not personally eat the fruit of the tree of the knowledge of good and evil, that sinful rebellion against God and the guilt associated with it were imputed to our accounts. Before we believed (in fact, from our mothers' wombs), God had declared us to be as sinful and as guilty as Adam because of Adam's disobedience (Rom. 5:12).

The Fall created a two-fold problem for us. First, God's justice demanded that we stand trial and be punished for our sins. Yet if we were to bear that punishment, it would mean that we would never be able to have fellowship with God. Second, long before sin ever entered the world, God's justice also demanded that we obey him perfectly so as to produce an active righteousness. Yet as creatures who were characterized by sin, wickedness and rebellion, we could not produce anything purely pleasing to God (Gen. 8:21; Jer. 17:9; Rom. 3:9-18). Even our best attempts at righteousness are stained with sin—that is why Isaiah says that even our good works are like dirty menstrual rags in God's sight. In terms of our checkbook illustration, we had plenty of debt—more than we could ever repay, due to our legal representative, Adam. But we also had zero credit (merit), and we were unable to conjure up any righteousness in and of ourselves.

But God solved both of those problems for us in Christ. First, he appointed Christ as our new legal, covenant representative—the "Last Adam" (1 Cor. 15:45). Christ went to the cross in order to solve the problem of our sin that deserved to be punished. How could he do that if the sin was *our* sin and not

Christ's sin? By imputation. God imputed our sins to Christ on the cross. Though we deserved eternal death in Hell at the end of history, that end came ahead of time for Christ on the cross. God legally considered Christ as if he were guilty of all—each and every one—of our sins (2 Cor. 5:21; Rom. 8:3; Gal. 3:13). So when he died on the cross, our sin was punished and paid for, so that God legally considered us as if we had never sinned. Thus, our account looked like this:

	Debit or Demerit	Credit or Merit	Balance
	nothing	nothing	nothing
Total:			nothing

But God's work of solving our two-fold problem was not finished with Christ's death. To be sure, his death was the culmination of a whole life full of obedience and characterized by obedience. Jesus perfectly obeyed his Father's righteous commands every single second of every single day. There is a good reason why Jesus was "born under the Law" (Gal. 4:4) rather than being born under "the Promise" (Gal. 3:15-18). He was "born under the Law" in order to be able to keep the Law perfectly, since the Law is based upon works (Gal. 3:12). Therefore, what Jesus rightly deserved was life, not death. God did not leave His only-begotten Son in the grave. Because he obeyed perfectly—even when it meant death on the cross—because he pleased his Father, Jesus was raised from the dead by the power of God. God justified Jesus (1 Tim. 3:16). In other words, God declared Jesus to be righteous because Jesus truly was (and is) righteous, in and of his human nature. That is why Jesus could pray in the Garden of Gethsemane, "I have glorified Thee upon the earth, completing the work which Thou gavest me to do. Now glorify Thou me with Thyself with the glory which I had with Thee before the world existed" (John 17:4, 5). Jesus did not trust someone outside of himself to obey *for him*. In other words, he was not justified by faith. Instead, it was on the basis of Jesus' own obedience to God's Law that his Father declared him to be righteous. Therefore, in one final act of imputation, God credited Christ's righteousness to believers so that he considers us to be as perfectly righteous as Jesus. Now our account looks like this:

	Debit or Demerit	Credit or Merit	Balance
	forgiven	The righteousness of Christ	The righteousness of Christ
Total:			righteous or justified

The righteousness in the credit or merit column is not from us. It comes to us from outside ourselves. In is not as though Jesus helps us to be good people who please God by what we do. It is *Jesus* who pleases God by what he already did, and God imputes what Jesus did, to you and me. By imputing Christ's righteousness to us, God is legally (justly, fairly) able to declare us to be righteous, even though in our own personal, daily experience, we know that we are wicked. That is why the Apostle Paul says, in Romans 4:5, "But to the one who does not work, but trusts Him who justifies the wicked, his faith is credited as righteousness." This is precisely why Protestants in the sixteenth century coined the phrase *simul iustus et peccator*: simultaneously just/righteous and sinful. Paul doesn't say that God justifies those who deserve to be declared just in and of themselves—he doesn't say that God justifies those who "are enabled to become covenant keepers,"[18] or who "persevere in *doing the will of God*"[19]. He says that God justifies the *wicked* who trust Christ. So "our" righteousness before God is actually Christ's righteousness imputed to our account. That is why the Reformers called it an

[18] Shepherd, Norman. *The Call of Grace*. (Phillipsburg: P&R, 2000), 57.

[19] Ibid., 49. (italics Shepherd's)

"alien righteousness." This alien righteousness is what Paul is talking about in Philippians 3:9, where he admits that he does not have "a righteousness which comes from the Law, but rather through faith in Christ, the righteousness from God, by faith."

After hearing this from the Reformers, the Roman Catholic church issued official statements toward the end of the sixteenth century, calling the Pauline doctrine of justification a "legal fiction." In other words, the Roman Catholic church was accusing the Reformers (and Paul) of calling God unjust. As Rome saw it, God could not justly or with any sense of fairness, declare a person righteous if he or she were actually sinful. Such a (legal) declaration would be fictitious, or untrue, Rome reasoned. Hence, the Roman Catholic church consciously and officially became legalistic and moralistic. They said that we are justified by a combination of our faith, our works and Christ's works—his works making up for the shortcomings in our own works. Even though Roman Catholic theology has a place for "credit" or "merit" in its doctrine of justification, it has no place for the covenant representation of Adam and Christ. Therefore, legalism and moralism come rushing in, in order to help us represent ourselves before God (yet, with the help of Christ).

Sadly, many contemporary Protestants—even those who would identify themselves with Reformation theology—are embracing and teaching doctrines of justification that are not substantially different from those of the Roman Catholic church. They do this not because of any affection for the errors that they perceive in Rome. Instead, they believe similarly to Rome about justification because they have begun to think like Rome: subtly blending or confusing faith and works as *both* being involved in how we are right with God. Of course, such well-intentioned brothers and sisters believe their positions to be the opposite of Rome's because Rome believes in merit as a biblical category for justification, while they claim to reject merit altogether. Yet by denying merit as a category, they have opened the floodgates for legalism and moralism. How? Because if our right standing—our righteousness before God—does not depend on the actions of our covenant representative, then it must depend on us. If that is true, then it means that the blessing of eternal life is *conditioned* upon our obedience, perseverance and faithfulness so that our works are the cause of our receiving, inheriting and entering eternal life.

However, faithful men before us had already thought through the kind of confusion and mixture of faith and works that these people are believing and teaching. To the question, "How does faith justify a sinner in the sight of God?" they replied,

> Faith justifies a sinner in the sight of God, ***not because*** of those other graces which do always accompany it, or *of good works that are the fruits of it* (Gal. 3:11; Rom. 3:28), nor as if the grace of faith, or any act thereof, were imputed to him for his justification (Rom. 4:5; 10:10), but only as it is an instrument by which he receiveth and applies Christ and his righteousness (John 1:12; Phil. 3:9; Gal. 2:16).[20]

So not only can we not please God by our pathetic, sin-stained obedience and faithfulness (Rom. 3:23)—we cannot even please God by our faith.

You see, faith and works are not simply two aspects of the same thing. They are two competing instruments by which we may please God. By the instrument of works, we could please God ourselves—if our works weren't stained with sin. By the instrument of faith, we may receive the righteousness of someone *else's* works as if they were our own. That is exactly how we are justified by faith *alone*. The apostle Paul is fond of listing opposites: *either*

---

[20] Westminster Larger Catechism, Question & Answer 73. Emphasis mine.

justification *or* condemnation (Rom. 5:15-19); *either* blessing *or* curse (Gal. 3:8-10); *either* the Promise *or* the Law (Gal. 3:18); *either* grace-faith *or* works (Rom. 3:28; 11:6; Gal. 3:2, 5, 11, 12). We are right with God *either* by faith *or* by works, but not by both. Paul is clear that we are right with God by faith and not by works. Yet our faith is not reward-able in and of itself. It is not as though we are such good people that God is impressed with our faith—for even our faith is God's demerited gift to us (Eph. 2:8, 9). Christ's righteousness pleases God, and we receive his righteousness—imputed to us as our own—the same way a beggar receives food: with outstretched hands. Faith is like outstretched hands, simply receiving and holding onto Christ—the only one who pleases God.

This is why the Heidelberg Catechism answers the question, "How are you right with God?" this way:

> Only by true faith in Jesus Christ (Rom. 3:21-25; Gal. 2:16; Eph. 2:8, 9; Phil. 3:9): that is, although my conscience accuses me, that I have grievously sinned against all the commandments of God, and have never kept any of them (Rom. 3:9-10), and am still prone always to all evil (Rom. 7:23); yet God, without any merit of mine (Titus 3:5), of mere grace (Rom. 3:24; Eph. 2:8), grants and imputes to me the perfect satisfaction (1 John 2:2), righteousness and holiness of Christ (1 John 2:1; Rom. 4:4-5; II Cor. 5:19); as if I had never committed nor had any sins, and had myself accomplished all the obedience which Christ has fulfilled for me (II Cor. 5:21); if only I accept such benefit with a believing heart (John 3:18; Rom. 3:28; 10:10).

Therefore, Protestants insist that justification comes by faith alone in Christ alone—and that our good works are the *result* of our justification. B. B. Warfield, the great systematic theologian of Old Princeton put it best when he said,

> "Justification by Faith, we see, is not to be set in
> contradiction to justification by Works. It is set in
> contradiction only to justification by Our Works. It
> is justification by Christ's Works."[21]

Some would fear that in saying all of this, I am denying that
Christians should do good works or obey what God commands.
Traditionally, someone who has rejected good works in any way,
shape or form has been called an *antinomian*. It comes from two
Greek words "anti" (against) and "nomos" (law—in this case, God's
law). Therefore, it refers to someone who does not believe that we
should observe what God commands. But that is not at all what
Paul meant, nor is it what the Reformers meant, nor is it what I
mean. I believe that the Bible teaches that works are indeed
necessary. But they are necessary as the *fruit* or *evidence* of faith and
justification. Or, in terms of our previous illustration about
Cameron and Bob, justification is the *cause* while the good works
are the *effects*.

In the world of theology, this is expressed as the relationship
between justification and sanctification. While justification means
to be legally declared righteous on the basis of Christ's obedience,
sanctification means a process of being set apart and *made* holy (or
conformed to the image of Christ) by the power and work of the
Holy Spirit. Sanctification is not the cause of justification. In other
words, sanctification does not cause us to be right with God. Only
justification causes us to be right with God. But justification and
sanctification never exist apart from each other. If you truly have
one, then you truly have the other because both are benefits that
Christ has earned for us. Therefore, if you are justified, then
sanctification will be the necessary result or effect because you
belong to Christ. As we examine the biblical covenants, we will

---

[21] B. B. Warfield, *Selected Shorter Writings, Vol. I*, "Justification by Faith, Out of
Date" ed. John E. Meeter (Phillipsburg: P&R Publishing, 2001), 283.

begin to see this difference: many in Christendom say we must be sanctified before we are justified, while the Bible says that Christ has earned our right standing with God and is bringing us into conformity to his image by his Spirit.

What Are You Talking About?

2

In the Beginning: Covenant and Creation

In the Beginning

Stories are best told from the beginning. We know this because God tells the story of His kingdom and His people from the beginning in Genesis 1:1. His story has a beginning, a middle and an end (or, more precisely, a completion or fulfillment). That is why all other stories have beginnings, middles and ends. After all, it just doesn't make any sense to begin a story in the middle. If you started in the middle, you would be confused: Who are the characters? Where did they come from? Where are they going? Why are they doing what they are doing? What is the story about? When is the story set? How will you know when the story has reached an appropriate conclusion? It doesn't make any sense to begin a story in the middle because that is not how God has ordered His creation. He has declared the end from the beginning (Is. 46:10) because He *is* the beginning, the Alpha, the first—the architect—as well as the end, the Omega, the last (Rev. 22:13)—the consummator (or the one who brings His creation to His intended fulfillment). Therefore, since we are His creatures—part of his beginning-middle-end creation—then we were created to understand stories in terms of beginnings, middles and ends.

Many people begin with the story of the covenant with Abraham since it is an important instance of covenant. But anyone who is familiar with the Bible knows that it does not begin with Abraham. The Bible begins with creation, and Adam is the major human character in the story of creation. If we begin with Abraham, then the part of the story that introduces the characters, sets the stage for the plot line and even foretells of the climax and fulfillment is brushed aside. Yet it is vitally important to the rest of the story of God's kingdom and covenants. Since the apostle Paul makes so many comparisons between Adam and Christ, then what we believe about the Father's covenant with Adam will (or should) affect what we believe about the Father's covenant with Christ, the Last Adam (1 Cor. 15:45).

As the beginning of the story, the covenant of creation with Adam will make sense out of the covenant of grace that comes after

47

the Fall. In fact, if we don't understand the first covenant, we won't be able to understand the rest of the covenants. If we misunderstand that original covenant, we will misunderstand the Gospel that is fully revealed in the New Covenant. Therefore, we will need to explore three main things. First, we will look at the biblical evidence for creation being covenantal. After all, if there was no covenant in the beginning, then there is nothing to relate the beginning to the later covenants. Second, we will see what the Bible has to say about whether the first covenant was one of works or of grace. We will see how vital it is that we understand the covenant of creation as a covenant of works. Third, we will examine the biblical evidence that indicates that Adam was supposed to have earned Heaven and the New Creation. This is what relates all of the biblical covenants to each other: they all work together toward the common goal of eternal life in the New Heavens and the New Earth. Nothing less than the Gospel, delivered to us by the apostles, is at stake.

HOW DO WE KNOW THAT CREATION WAS COVENANTAL?

In the beginning, God created the Heavens and the earth (Gen. 1:1). In other words, as Paul tells us, "by Him, everything was created in the Heavens and upon the earth—the visible things and the invisible things—whether supernatural powers or ruling powers or dominions or authorities" (Col. 1:16). For some reason, we tend to think of Heaven as being as eternal as God Himself. But Paul says that God created even that invisible realm. He not only created the visible heavens (the starry, planet-filled skies) and the visible earth, but He also created the invisible Heaven to be the ultimate location of His kingdom.

But before God dwelt with His human creatures in His ultimate, Heavenly kingdom, he placed Adam and Eve in a "miniature" visible-version of His kingdom in the Garden of Eden. Some would say that the first covenant began when God

48

approached Adam with the terms of the covenant in Genesis chapter 2. But that would mean that there was a period of time in history, from the absolute beginning (Gen. 1:1) until Genesis 2, in which there was primal nature that was not governed by God's covenant. However, the Bible clearly indicates that creation was covenantal from the words "Let there be."

1. Old Testament References[22]: Who can interpret God's Word better than God Himself? Of course, no one can. Therefore, when other portions of the Bible talk about, or shed light on a particular passage, we should begin our thinking with the interpretation that God gives us. In this case, the passage we are thinking about is Genesis chapters 1 and 2. The good news is that God has provided other places in the Scriptures that help us to interpret the full significance and importance of creation. Probably the clearest biblical reference to God's covenant of creation is found in the book of the prophet Jeremiah. In chapter 33 the prophet says,

> Thus says the LORD: If any of you could break my covenant with the day and my covenant with the night, so that day and night would not come at their appointed time, only then could my covenant with my servant David be broken, so that he would not have a son to reign on his throne, and my covenant with my ministers the Levites... Thus says the LORD: Only if I had not established my covenant with day and night and the ordinances of heaven and earth, would I reject the offspring of Jacob and of my servant David and not choose any of his descendants as rulers over the offspring of Abraham, Isaac, and Jacob. For I will restore their fortunes, and will have mercy upon them. (Jer. 33:20, 21, 25, 26 NRSV)

---

[22] Most of these references were learned and taken from Meredith G. Kline's book *Kingdom Prologue*, (Overland Park: Two Age Press, 2000).

In these verses, the LORD is making a promise to believing Israelites (Jews who were trusting in the promised Messiah). His promise is that they will undoubtedly be saved. But he makes an analogy or comparison between His covenant with David and his covenant with creation: If He made a covenant with creation, then He made covenants with Abraham and David; If the covenant with creation can be broken (if the day and the night stop coming at their appointed times) then the covenants with Abraham and David can be broken (Abraham's descendants in the faith will not inherit the *ultimate* Promised Land; David's son will not sit on the throne). But nobody doubts that the day and the night will come at their appointed times, and so no believer should doubt that Christ now sits on David's throne, reigning as our King. Neither should we doubt the covenant of saving grace that God has made with us as Abraham's descendants in the faith. Jeremiah 33:20-26 may very well be referring to the covenant of common grace that God made with all of creation after the flood. If so, the analogy between the covenant with the post-flood creation and the covenant with Abraham would work better because they would both be operating on the principle of grace. But even if that is what Jeremiah 33:20-26 is about, that does not rule out the fact that Genesis 1 and 2 are in the background. It is no accident that in Jeremiah 33:20, the prophet borrows from the language of Genesis 1:3-5.

Jeremiah records almost exactly the same thing in chapter 31:

> Thus says the LORD, who gives the sun for light by day, and the fixed order of the moon and the stars for light by night, who stirs up the sea so that its waves roar; The LORD of hosts is His name: "If this fixed order departs from before Me," declares the LORD, "Then the offspring of Israel also shall cease from being a nation before Me forever." Thus says the LORD, "If the heavens above can be measured, and the foundations of the earth searched out below,

then I will also cast off all the offspring of Israel for all that they have done," declares the LORD. (Jer. 31:35-37 NRSV)

This time the word "covenant" does not appear. But the meaning is the same as Jeremiah 33:20-26—God has made covenants with creation and with Israel (Lev. 26:42-45; Deut. 29:1). Therefore the sun, moon, day, night, sea and heavens will keep their place and fulfill their function, and God will always have His people who are called by His name. So it is clear that God speaks of creation as being covenantal. In both Jeremiah 31:35-37 and 33:20-26, He refers to the days of creation in Genesis 1 and says that He made a covenant with them. There was no time between "Let there be" and the beginning of the first covenant.

There is one more clear reference to the covenant of creation in the Old Testament, even though it only mentions Adam as the representative of all creation. This time it is the prophet Hosea who helps us to interpret Genesis 1 and 2: "But they (Israel), like Adam[23], have transgressed the covenant..." (Hosea 6:7). Hosea could not have said this about Israel if Adam (and the creation of which he was a part) was not also under a covenant. Therefore, Adam and creation were under God's covenant of creation.

2. God's Word is His Bond: "In this, God, wanting to demonstrate even more clearly to the heirs of the promise the unchangeableness of His purpose, gave His guarantee by swearing an oath, so that by two unchangeable things—for it is impossible for God to lie—we would have strong encouragement, we who have taken refuge to seize the hope that is set before us" (Heb. 6:17, 18). The author of Hebrews says that there were *two* things by which

---

[23] There is some debate about whether the Hebrew word *adam* should be rendered "Adam" or simply "man." I hold that the rendering "man" would create an unnecessary tautology and introduce a nature-grace dualism that is foreign to Scripture.

Abraham, and we, can be encouraged. The first thing was the promise that he made to Abraham in Genesis 12. The second thing was the oath that he swore to Abraham on top of that promise in Genesis 15. The promise was enough to make it a sure thing. In other words, when God speaks, His speech not only provides interpretation, definition and meaning, but whatever He says will come to pass beyond any shadow of a doubt.

Therefore, in the beginning when God said, "Let there be..." he was swearing an oath, that what He said would certainly happen. Not only that, but He was also swearing to uphold and govern His good creation. Remember that oaths are so essential to covenants that when we encounter an oath in the Bible, we can be sure that we are reading about a covenant. So by the very act of creating, God was also entering into covenant with creation.

3. Dual Sanctions—Blessing and Curse: Just like the oaths God swore in Genesis 1, the sanctions—or consequences—that God offered to Adam for his obedience and with which He threatened Adam for his disobedience show that creation was covenantal. God was *enforcing* His covenant. After all, where you find the *essential* "stuff" or "ingredients" of a covenant, you can be sure that you have found a covenant.

The most obvious consequence of the covenant of creation is the threat that God made to Adam in Genesis 2:17—"But from the Tree of the Knowledge of Good and Evil you shall not eat, for in the day that you eat from it you will certainly die." This was the curse sanction of the covenant of creation. It should be clear that when the *future* or the *outcome* of a covenant is under discussion, there must be a covenant already in existence in order for an outcome to be possible.

The second and opposite sanction or consequence is not so obvious. That is why it is easily missed—but it is still there. If the first sanction was the curse sanction—the threat of Death—then the second sanction was the blessing sanction: the offer of Life. It is interesting to note that both sanctions are attached to trees. God attached the curse sanction to the Tree of the Knowledge of Good and Evil, and He attached the blessing sanction to the Tree of Life.

There are two ways that we know that the Tree of Life held out the offer of ultimate Life with God in His Kingdom. The first is the presence of the Tree of Life in the Bible. It only shows up in two places: the original creation and the New Creation.[24] Genesis 2:9 tells us that the Tree of Life was in the midst of the Garden of Eden. After the first few chapters of Genesis, the only other place that the Tree of Life appears in the Bible is the book of Revelation in the context of the New Creation:

> ...and on that side [of the river] was the Tree of Life producing twelve fruits every month, giving its fruit each month, and the leaves of the Tree were for the healing of the nations. (Rev. 22:2)

The second way we know that the Tree of Life held out the offer of ultimate Life in the Kingdom of God is the way the Bible speaks about it as the way of entrance into that Kingdom. After Adam had disobeyed God and broken the covenant of creation, God took away Adam's access to the Tree of Life:

> And the LORD God said, "Behold, the man has become like one from among us, "knowing" good and evil; and now, lest he reach out his hand and take from the Tree of Life, and eat, and live eternally—and so the LORD God sent him away from the garden of Eden..." (Gen. 3:22, 23)

---

[24] The phrase "Tree of Life" does appear a handful of times in the book of Proverbs, but there it is used figuratively for "blessing." The occurrences of the "Tree of Life" in Genesis and Revelation refer to a real tree in real time-space history.

On the other end of history, at the end of the Bible, God speaks the same way about the Tree of Life:

> He who has an ear, let him hear what the Spirit says to the churches: "To the One who is victorious I will grant to Him to eat from the Tree of Life which is in the Paradise of God." (Rev. 2:7)

> Blessed are they who wash their robes so that they might have the right to the Tree of Life and might enter into the gates of the City. (Rev. 22:14)

So the Bible speaks of the Tree of Life as being a real tree that represents access to eternal life in the ultimate, heavenly Kingdom of God. This is what was offered to Adam *if* he obeyed God perfectly. In conclusion then, the Tree of the Knowledge of Good and Evil and the Tree of Life—along with what both trees threatened or offered *as the future outcome of the covenant*—shows that there was a covenant in the beginning.

HOW DO WE KNOW THAT THE COVENANT OF CREATION WAS A COVENANT OF WORKS?

There are many people who would be willing to say that before the Fall, God dealt with Adam on the basis of Adam's works. However, some of those people are not willing to say that God dealt with Adam *exclusively* on the basis of Adam's works. They also want to say that before the Fall, God also dealt with Adam on the basis of His free grace.

Yet confusing as it may be, it is important to keep in mind the biblical definitions of works, merit and grace that we considered in chapter 1. No matter how much anyone says it and no matter how sincerely anyone believes it, there can be no grace before the Fall. Why? Because grace is God's favor *in spite of* our sin—*in spite of*

Adam's violation of His covenant. So to say that there was grace before the Fall is to say that Adam had sinned before the Fall and needed God's favor to help him accomplish what he had made himself unable to accomplish (i.e., keeping the covenant). To say that there was grace before the Fall is to say that Adam violated the covenant before he and Eve ate from the Tree of the Knowledge of Good and Evil. In other words, to say that there was grace before the Fall means that Adam fell *before* the Fall—and that would mean that God was *wrong* when He looked at His creation (including Adam) *before the Fall* and declared it "very good" (Gen. 1:31).

The implications of saying that there was grace before the fall are horrifying. God gives us life in salvation by *grace*. What we *deserve* is His wrath because we have fallen with Adam and offended Him (Rom. 5:12; Mat. 25:41). Yet instead of pouring out His wrath upon us (which would have been fair and just), He chose to pour out His wrath for us on His own Son (Rom. 5:8; 2 Cor. 5:21). Not only that, but He has counted Christ's righteous obedience as if it were our own righteous obedience—*in spite of our sin* (Phil. 3:9; Rom. 3:21, 22; Gal. 2:16). That is *how* God "freely gave" us life in salvation. It is free to *us*, but it came at great cost to God. That is *not* how God "freely gave" life to Adam on the very first day of his existence. If it *were* how God freely gave life to Adam, we would have to say that Adam was created far from "very good" (Gen. 1:31). If that was how God freely gave him life, we would have to say that God created Adam *just like we are today*: fallen, wicked (Rom. 4:5), sinful (Phil. 3:12), and the list could go on. In the words of the Apostle Paul, "May it never be!" (Rom. 6:2).

So there was no grace in the covenant of creation. But did God deal with Adam on the basis of works and merit? There are good, solid, biblical reasons for believing that God did hold Adam *personally* responsible for producing *perfect* obedience. So let's see what the Bible has to say.

1. Creation in the Image of God: Genesis 1:26 and 27 tells us that God made man in His own image. Entire books have been written on what it means to be made in the image of God.[25] So we will leave a long and complete exploration of that subject to those other books. The important point, for our purposes, is that Adam was to imitate God, to be like God—at least as much as an earthly son can be like his Heavenly Father.

So what did God do that Adam could imitate? At the end of His work of creation, God surveyed all that He had made and judicially declared that it was "very good" (Gen. 1:31). Since His work was very good, "on the seventh day, God completed the work that He had done, and He rested on the seventh day from all the works that He had done. So God blessed the seventh day and set it apart as sanctified because on it God rested from all the works He made during creation" (Gen. 2:2, 3). God did His work perfectly. Therefore, He *deserved* the "rest."[26]

In the same way, Adam was to do the work that God had given him to do—not only abstaining from the Tree of the Knowledge of Good and Evil (Gen. 2:17), but also ruling over creation (Gen. 1:26-30), producing a human race to inherit the ultimate Kingdom of God (Gen. 2:24; Eph. 5:22-33—esp. vv. 31 and 32) and rebuking Satan and protecting the miniature Kingdom in Eden from Satan (Gen. 3:1-6; Luke 4:1-13). The reward for Adam's good works would be entrance into the same rest that God had entered into on the seventh day. We know this because the Last Adam, Jesus Christ, entered God's rest (Heb. 4:10)—and if the Last

---

[25] One of the best of these is Meredith G. Kline's book *Images of the Spirit* (Eugene: Wipf and Stock, 1999).

[26] This language of "work" and "rest" in the early chapters of Genesis should be understood in terms of merit and reward. God is not a man, that He should become exhausted by His "labors." Therefore the "rest" that He entered ought to be understood in terms of the reward that He justly or fairly attached to His good work. This will become clearer as we examine what the book of Hebrews has to say about this passage in Genesis.

Adam did it, the first Adam *should have* done it. The bottom line, then, is that Adam's good works would have earned him (and us) the right to enter into God's eternal Sabbath rest because his good works would have been meritorious (or worthy). God rested because His good work was complete and acceptable. Adam, made in God's image, would have entered God's rest if his work were like God's: good, complete and acceptable to God.

2. The Two Adams of the Apostle Paul: In chapter 1, we looked at the comparison and contrast that the apostle Paul makes between Adam and Christ in Romans 5:12-18 and 1 Corinthians 15:40-50. We won't repeat everything that we have already said, but these passages cannot be emphasized enough. It is not only important to recognize that Paul is making a parallel between Adam and Christ, but it is also vital to recognize how Adam and Christ are being *contrasted* as well as how they are being *compared*.

1 Corinthians 15:45 provides the crystal-clear parallel by first referring to "the first man Adam" and then referring to "the Last Adam." There is no doubt that "the Last Adam" is Jesus Christ, because who else "became the life-giving Spirit" except Jesus at Pentecost when He sent His Holy Spirit to be His abiding presence with the Church? Who else is from heaven except Jesus, the incarnate Son of God (1 Cor. 15:47)? It is no accident, then, that Paul calls Jesus "the Last Adam."

If 1 Corinthians 15:45 is the clearest parallel and connection between Adam and Christ, then Romans 5:14 comes in a close second. There Paul says that Adam was a "type of the One who was to come." But we don't usually use the word "type" that way in English. So what is Paul talking about when he calls Adam a "type" of Christ? Perhaps the simplest way to describe a type is *an earthly anticipation* (e.g., a person, an object, a kingdom, etc.) *of a heavenly reality*. This is supported by 1 Corinthians 15:47—there is a man from earth (Adam), and there is a man from heaven (Christ). Paul calls one "the first man Adam" and he calls the other "the Last

Adam." Adam was the type and Christ is the antitype (or fulfillment).

But there is obviously a difference between the first Adam and the Last Adam. The difference is clear: Adam sinned, but Christ obeyed His Father perfectly. When Paul *contrasts* Adam and Christ in the New Testament, he is explaining the importance and significance of that difference. Adam's violation earned covenant breaking, sin, guilt, condemnation and eternal death in Hell for humanity. Christ's obedience earned covenant keeping, righteousness, forgiveness, justification and eternal life in Heaven for the elect.

Yet the differences between Adam and Christ would make no sense unless there was some common point of comparison between them. Another way to put it is that apples are different from oranges, and as the cliché goes, "you can't compare apples with oranges." They are different, and that's all there is to it. But you can compare apples with apples. An apple is supposed to be sweet, crunchy and juicy. Because of those common points of comparison, you can eat two apples and discover that one is a bad apple (rotten, wormy and mushy) while the other is a good apple—the way an apple is supposed to be.

The point is that the differences between Adam and Christ make sense because they do share a common point of comparison between them. They were both related to the Father by a covenant. Both Adam and Christ were under a covenant in which life and death were at stake—not only for themselves individually, but for humanity as well. Both of them were threatened with ultimate death if they disobeyed and both of them were offered ultimate life if they obeyed. That explains why Paul calls them "the first man Adam" and "the Last Adam," and then goes on to describe Adam as the bad covenant representative who broke the covenant he was involved in—introducing sin, death, and condemnation into the world—while Christ is the good covenant representative who earned righteousness, forgiveness, justification and eternal life for His people.

The apostle Paul's theology of the two Adams is important for understanding what kind of covenant Adam was involved in because whatever is true for one Adam is true for the other Adam as well. If God gave the reward of the covenant to Christ on the basis of grace, then he would have also dealt with Adam on the basis of grace, too. But if grace is God's *demerited* favor, His blessing *in spite of* sin, then to say that God dealt with Christ on the basis of grace is to say that God dealt with Christ as a sinner who deserved God's wrath. Even the suggestion of such a thing ought to strike horror in our very beings. The New Testament is clear that Jesus never sinned, but was perfectly obedient. So Jesus did not obtain the covenant blessings by grace.

But did He obtain the covenant blessings by works? Yes, He did. He not only bore the punishment that we deserved for our own sins, but He actively obeyed God's law on our behalf as well. In fact, He did His work so well that He was able to say to His Father, "I have glorified Thee on the earth by completing the work that Thou gavest me to do; now glorify Thou me, Father, with Thyself, with the glory I had with Thee before the world existed " (John 17:4, 5). The resurrection was the reward that Christ *deserved*. God sent His Son into the world to save everyone whom He had given to His Son (John 6:37-40; 10:25-29)—His Son was obedient to the point of death, even death on a cross (Phil. 2:8)—and so His Son *deserved* the eternal life that he earned for the elect (Eph. 1:3-14). So if the Last Adam was under a covenant of works, then the first Adam must have been under a covenant of works as well.

3. The Nature of the Sanctions: It is interesting to note that both sanctions or consequences of the covenant of creation—eternal death associated with eating from the Tree of the Knowledge of Good and Evil, and eternal life associated with eating from the Tree of Life—both sanctions were *conditional*. One was a *threat* and the other was an *offer*. God had not *guaranteed* either consequence as the *certain* outcome, because He had set up the covenant in such a way that Adam's obedience or disobedience would cause one of the consequences. Of course, God knows everything because He has planned and declared the end from the beginning (Is. 46:10; Ps. 139:16). But God had arranged the covenant so that Adam's obedience would cause his right to the Tree of Life while his disobedience would cause his eternal Death.

Since the future of the covenant depended upon what *Adam did*, that indicates that the original covenant of creation was a covenant of works.[27] In terms of the consequence in Genesis 2:17, Adam's disobedience would cause his own death because that is the worth or value (in this case, *demerit*) that God had attached to his disobedience. By the same token, Adam's obedience would have caused the right to eternal life with God in His Kingdom because that is the value (in this case, *merit*) that God had attached to his obedience.

The subject of the covenant sanctions also involves the question of how Adam would have been declared right with God (if he had not fallen). It involves the question of how Adam would have been justified. Why? Because in order for God to justly and fairly assign to Adam the covenant blessing or the covenant curse, He would have to make a judgment or a ruling on Adam's works: righteous or guilty. Adam would have to stand before God at the Final Judgment. Of course, we know what became of the covenant of creation. But fact still remains that if God's justice had demanded that Adam should enter the ultimate, heavenly Kingdom of God, it would have been because God had evaluated Adam's works and had declared them to be righteous in His sight. Adam

---

[27] Compare chapters 2 – 9 of volume 1 of Herman Witsius' book *Economy of the Covenants Between God and Man: Comprehending A Complete Body of Divinity*; also Francis Turretin's *Institutes of Elenctic Theology*, volume 1, topic 8, question 3 (pp. 574-578).

would have merited the future outcome of the covenant by his works because his works would have justified him (or made him right with God).

4. If There was no Grace, Then There *Must* have been Works: Since we have ruled out grace as a possibility before the Fall, works is the only other option. Why? Because the apostle Paul tells us that there are really only two options. In Galatians 3:18, Paul says "For if the inheritance comes by the Law, then it no longer comes by the Promise—but God graciously granted it to Abraham by the Promise." Earlier in Galatians, Paul had already explained that the Law was based on works (Gal. 3:12). So what he is saying in 3:18 is that the inheritance (eternal life in the Kingdom of God) comes either by our works or by God's grace—*but **not** both*. Since he says that it is *either* by the Law *or* by the Promise—*either* works *or* grace—then we can apply the logic of Galatians 3:18 to the covenant of creation like this: "For if the inheritance comes by the Law, then it no longer comes by the Promise"—God fairly or justly offered the inheritance to Adam by the Law—*therefore there was no Promise* (grace) *in the covenant of creation.*

Paul said the same thing in Romans 6:14—"For sin shall not master you because you are not under the Law, but under Grace." The 'but' in "not under the Law, *but* under Grace" is more forceful in the Greek. It draws a sharp contrast between things. The effect, then, is the same as the *either/or* contrast in Galatians 3:18. Since we are under grace, we are not under the Law. But since Adam was not under grace, he *was* under the Law. There simply is no third option.

But the clearest and most persuasive evidence comes from Romans 11:6—"and if by grace, then it is no longer by works—*otherwise grace would no longer be grace*" (emphasis mine). Here Paul uses the same either/or contrast that he used in the other two verses. But this time he adds an amazing conclusion: if works are involved as actions that are *worthy* of reward or punishment (i.e., meritorious), then grace is no longer God's favor *in spite of our sin.* God's favor is not *demerited* if we are meriting His favor by our works. So if works are involved, grace is not involved. For reasons mentioned earlier, grace was not involved in the covenant of creation. Therefore, on Paul's reasoning in Romans 11:6, God dealt with Adam on the basis of Adam's works in the covenant of creation.

HOW DO WE KNOW THAT ADAM WAS TO HAVE EARNED HEAVEN?

Most people seem to think that if Adam had obeyed God—if he had not fallen—then he would have simply continued to live forever on earth. But as we began to see as we looked at the two sanctions or future outcomes of the covenant of creation, the same old earthly life was not what was offered to Adam as the outcome of his obedience. This is where eschatology enters the picture: as early as Genesis 1:1. Heaven was created to be the realm in which the ultimate Kingdom of God would be located, and where God would reign over his human creatures—even as they reigned over the rest of the (at that point, New) creation. The apostle Paul refers to this when he talks about "this age" and "the age to come" in Eph. 1:21. "This age" began with this creation (Gen. 1 and 2) and continues on until the Final Judgment. "The age to come" is the New Creation and the Kingdom of God in its ultimate, Heavenly form. That "age to come" was what Adam looked forward to earning for himself, his wife and their children.

If most people seem to think that Adam would have lived forever on earth if he had obeyed, then most people also seem to think that Heaven is simply the conclusion to salvation. So it sounds strange to Protestants to say that Adam would have earned eternal life in Heaven for keeping the covenant. Since "eternal life" and "Heaven" are things we normally associate with salvation, then to say that Adam would have earned Heaven sounds as if we were saying that Adam needed to be saved *even before he fell.* Of course, that is *not* what we saying, nor is it what we mean—because it would contradict God's verdict, that His creation (including Adam and Eve) was "very good" (Gen. 1:31), and it would blur the biblical distinction between Creation and Redemption, making Redemption meaningless.

All we mean when we say that Adam would have earned eternal life in Heaven by keeping the covenant is that the ultimate Kingdom of God has *always* been the goal. The Kingdom was not only God's *purpose* in creation but it was His *model* for creation. Adam was the creature-king—made in the image of the Great King— ruling over the miniature kingdom of God in Eden for the purpose of earning the covenant blessing: having the New Creation clothed upon this creation. There are many reasons for believing this.

1. The Interpretation Given by the New Testament: We have already seen how both Adam and Christ are parallel to each other. They were involved in the same kind of covenant: a covenant of works in which they were to merit the outcome of the covenant by what they personally did. So, based on Romans 5:12-19 and 1 Corinthians 15:40-50, the simplest way to show that Adam should have earned Heaven for us, is to observe that Christ *did* earn Heaven for us. What the Last Adam accomplished, the first man Adam should have accomplished as well. Since Christ earned Heaven by His covenantal obedience, Adam should have earned Heaven by his covenantal obedience, too.

But another New Testament passage that compares Adam and Christ makes this point even more clearly.

> ...the husband is the head of the wife, as Christ also is the head of the church, He Himself *being* the Savior of the body. But as the church is subject to Christ, so also the wives ought to be to their husbands in everything. Husbands, love your wives,

just as Christ also loved the church and gave Himself up for her; that He might sanctify her, having cleansed her by the washing of water with the word, that He might present to Himself the church in all her glory, having no spot or wrinkle or any such thing; but that she should be holy and blameless. So husbands ought also to love their own wives as their own bodies. He who loves his own wife loves himself; for no one ever hated his own flesh, but nourishes and cherishes it, just as Christ also does the church, because we are members of His body. "For this cause a man shall leave his father and mother, and shall cleave to his wife; and the two shall become one flesh." This mystery is great; but I am speaking with reference to Christ and the church. (Eph. 5:23-32, NASB)

Though the apostle Paul does not mention Adam by name, he does refer to Adam by quoting Genesis 2:24. The context of Genesis 2:24 is the creation of the woman from Adam's rib. After putting Adam into a deep sleep, creating the woman from one of Adam's ribs and then presenting the woman to Adam as his helper, God declared, "For this cause a man shall leave his father and mother, and shall cleave to his wife; and the two shall become one flesh."

We usually hear this passage used to preach about marriage—and it is true that marriage does come from God joining Adam and Eve together. However, Paul's statement in Ephesians 5:32 is rich with eschatology because it makes the connection between Adam and Christ ("This mystery is great, but I am speaking with reference to Christ and the church"). He is talking about Adam because he quotes from the Genesis narrative about Adam (and his wife), but he goes on to say that what he is *really* talking about is Christ and the Church. There is the comparison and contrast between the First Adam and the Last Adam in Ephesians 5:31 and 32.

As we look back over the entire passage, we see the parallel in more detail. Adam parallels Christ, and Eve parallels the Church. Christ is the head of the Church who loves the Church, gave Himself for her and sanctifies her so that He can present her to Himself with no sin—holy and blameless. Since He is currently sanctifying us (cleansing us by the washing of water with the word), He will present us to Himself at the Last Day after the Final Judgment. On that Day, the Almighty Judge will find that we are holy and blameless because Christ not only bore our curse for our sins, but He also obeyed His Father perfectly to provide us with the righteousness we need to stand before Him. Except that before the Fall Eve did not need salvation from sin, that is how Adam was to have treated Eve (and all of their children). He was to have prepared her and all of their children for entrance into the ultimate Kingdom of God—so that when God came to judge Adam's work, he would find them all holy and blameless, worthy to live eternally with Him.

2. The Tree of Life: Most of the significance of the Tree of Life was worked out earlier in this chapter, but it never hurts to repeat it. Genesis 2:9 tells us that the Tree of Life was present in the Garden of Eden. But the life to which it referred was not the same as the life Adam was living in the Garden. We know this, of course, by the fact that the Tree of Life does not reappear in the Bible until the New Creation in the book of Revelation. The Tree of Life, then, is about eternal life in the ultimate Kingdom of God. It appears in the early chapters of Genesis in parallel with the Tree of the Knowledge of Good and Evil. Eternal death—the curse of the covenant of creation—was attached to eating from the Tree of the Knowledge of Good and Evil. Eternal life—the blessing of the covenant of creation—was attached to eating from the Tree of Life. If Adam earned eternal death by his disobedience in eating from the Tree of the Knowledge of Good and Evil, then he could have earned eternal life by his obedience and being given the right to eat from the Tree of Life.

3. The Sabbath Rest of God: We have already seen how Adam was to imitate God by doing the work that God gave him to do; and then, after God approved of his work, Adam was to enter into God's rest, too. But what does the seventh day of creation have to do with Heaven? It has everything to do with Heaven. In fact, the New Testament interprets that seventh day of rest as being Heaven itself.

Hebrews chapters 3 and 4 say this the clearest. The author of Hebrews even quotes Genesis 2:2—"...and He rested on the seventh day from all the works that He had done." Here is the passage in its context:

> Therefore, since a promise remains of entering His rest, let us fear lest any of you seem to have come short of it. For indeed the gospel was preached to us as well as to them; but the word which they heard did not profit them, not being mixed with faith in those who heard it. For we who have believed do enter that rest, as He has said:
>
> > "So I swore in My wrath,
> > 'They shall not enter My rest,' "
>
> although the works were finished from the foundation of the world. For He has spoken in a certain place of the seventh day in this way: "And God rested on the seventh day from all His works"; and again in this place: "They shall not enter My rest." Since therefore it remains that some must enter it, and those to whom it was first preached did not enter because of disobedience, again He designates a certain day, saying in David, "Today," after such a long time, as it has been said:
>
> > "Today, if you will hear His voice,
> > Do not harden your hearts."

For if Joshua had given them rest, then He would
not afterward have spoken of another day. There
remains therefore a rest for the people of God. For
he who has entered His rest has himself also ceased
from his works as God did from His. (Heb. 4:1-10,
NKJV)

There are several places in this passage in which the author
identifies the seventh day of God's rest as being an *eternal day*, that
is, Heaven. First, he says that *we who believe* enter God's rest...*even
though* God's works were finished from the foundation of the world.
In other words, God did not rest for a short period of time after He
finished the work of creation. God is still resting from His work.
The logic would remain the same if we turned the sentence around
to read, "*even though* God's works were finished from the foundation
of the world, *we who believe* enter God's rest." We enter the *same rest*
that God entered when He finished creating; and we know that the
"rest" being spoken of in Hebrews 4 is the seventh day of creation
because in the very next verse (Heb. 4:4) the author quotes Genesis
2:2.

But he goes on to say that there are some who have not yet
entered into God's eternal, seventh-day rest—not yet, but they *will*.
Since it has been such a long time since God entered that rest—and
since there are some people who will still be entering it, too—God
set aside a certain day, calling it "Today." Back in David's time,
God called Israel to faith and repentance saying "Today, if you will
hear His voice, do not harden your hearts" (Ps. 95:7). The author of
Hebrews quotes Psalm 95:7 because God is calling us to the same
faith and repentance. The Israelites who trusted in the promised
Messiah entered into God's seventh-day rest, and *we* who are called
by God to faith in Christ *also* enter into that same rest.

Finally, he says, "he who has entered His rest has himself
also ceased from his works as God *did* from His." But who has
entered God's rest just like God did? Jesus did. That is why Joshua

is mentioned. The first Joshua did not provide the ultimate rest of God's seventh day for Israel. But the New and Better Joshua—Jesus Christ the Righteous—has provided that ultimate rest for us because He has entered in before us. He entered that rest when He ascended into Heaven. This provides yet another parallel between Adam and Christ. We can confidently say that Adam was supposed to have earned God's Heavenly seventh-day rest because Christ, the Last Adam *has* entered that rest.

CONCLUSION

So Adam, and the rest of creation, was created very good. He and the rest of creation were also created in covenant with God. That covenant was a covenant of works in which Adam's obedience would merit Heaven and his disobedience would demerit Hell. That is not because Adam was so arrogant that he thought his good works could bring *more* glory to God than God already had. Nor is it because God was some kind of cold-hearted, uncaring, unloving employer who wanted to take advantage of Adam. The covenant of creation was a covenant of works because *that is how God designed that covenant* as Adam's Heavenly Father. God sovereignly decided that Adam's obedience *merited* (was worth) Heaven and that his disobedience *demerited* (was worth) Hell. This no more detracts from the father-son relationship between God and Adam than the illustration from chapter one detracted from the father-son relationship between Bob and Cameron.

To deny that the covenant of creation was a covenant of works is an attack on the Gospel of salvation by grace alone through faith alone because of Christ alone. Earlier in the chapter we saw that if God gave Adam life by grace at creation—*before the Fall*—then God gave Adam life in spite of Adam's sin, wickedness and rebellion *before the Fall* (and that makes no sense). But seeing the covenant of creation as gracious also affects what we believe about Christ, the Last Adam. For if Adam was under a covenant of grace, then the Last Adam would also have been under a covenant of grace. But if grace is more than *undeserved* favor—if grace is also receiving the outcome of the covenant *in spite of what you do deserve*—then God the Father could have said to Christ, "Because of your active obedience in keeping My law and your passive obedience in submitting to death on a cross, I know that you deserve the resurrection and eternal life in My ultimate Kingdom for you and your people... but since this is all based on grace, you (and your people) have to go to Hell because that's what you get in spite of what you deserve!" How truly horrifying it is to say that God dealt with the first man Adam on the basis of grace.

You can probably see the relevance of this covenant for your own life. Adam was supposed to have merited eternal life in the Kingdom of God for you. Your eternal destiny was in his hands. If he obeyed, you would enter into Heaven with him. But if he disobeyed, you would enter into Hell with him. In other words, the covenant of creation gives meaning and significance to your life. You are not merely looking at this story in your Bible as a mere spectator. You are a participant in the story, because what Adam did, he did *for you*. If we were to diagram the history of God's covenantal administration of His Kingdom so far, it would look like this:

In the absolute beginning (Gen. 1:1)...

...God created the invisible Heavens as well as the visible heavens and the visible earth (Gen. 1:1ff.; Col. 1:16).

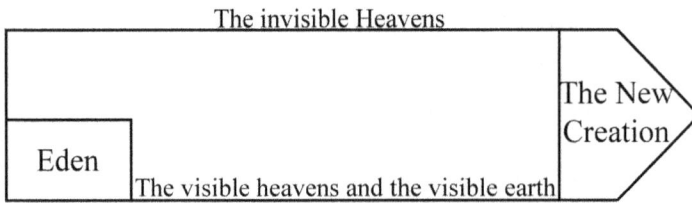

The invisible Heavens

Eden

The visible heavens and the visible earth

The New Creation

Because Adam was created in God's image—because of the comparison between Adam and Christ—because of the God-ordained significance of the Tree of the Knowledge of Good and Evil as well as the Tree of Life and because the covenant was *not* based upon grace—Adam was to have merited Heaven for us as our first covenant representative.

3

Covenant *Before* Creation: The Covenant Between the Father, Son and Holy Spirit

Covenant *Before* Creation

We all know how the covenant of creation turned out. Though the first man Adam should have earned the ultimate Kingdom of God for us, he merited the curse of the covenant instead. Rather than life, he earned death. Instead of producing righteousness and obedience, he produced sin and violation. Rather than justification, he justly received condemnation. To Adam (and to us) it might appear that the eternal life of the New Creation in the Heavenly Kingdom of God was no longer a possibility.

Thankfully, the reward of the covenant was not only still a possibility, but for God's people it was and is absolutely sure. This is not because God is a "softy" who decided to go back on His justice by not giving Adam and humanity the covenant curse that was merited. No, God is still just. But the reward of Heaven is totally secured for us by the second man (1 Cor. 15:47)–the Last Adam (1 Cor. 15:45). Somehow, the Fall was part of God's plan. In fact, He had already planned the remedy in eternity past. That is why this is the tale of two Adams.

Remember from Romans 5:12-19 and 1 Corinthians 15:40-50, that we do not merely stand before God as "rugged individuals." By God's own design, He has appointed a representative for us. Theologians call the biblical teaching about God's representatives for humanity "federal theology." That is because the word "federal" has to do with a representative form of government. So God deals with us based upon the actions and accomplishments of our representative.

Of course, when we consider what our first representative, Adam, did for us, we may wonder how that broken covenant of works might be repaired. After all, what can *we* do? Our nature (as human beings) is now sinful as a result of the Fall, so we can't please God ourselves. And we certainly can't pridefully imagine that we could go back in time and do a better job than Adam. But that is precisely the point. The original covenant of works cannot be repaired. But that does not spell despair, because *another* covenant of works *can* be kept by a second representative: the eternal Son of God who would become flesh—become one of us—so that he could keep the covenant of works *as* one of us. The three persons of the Trinity covenanted together to succeed where Adam failed. The Father sent the Son to fulfill the covenant that Adam violated, while the Holy Spirit was sent to apply the Son's accomplishment to God's chosen people. In this chapter, we will explore the biblical evidence for this eternal covenant and we will also look at the differences between it and the Covenant of Grace.

HOW DO WE KNOW THAT THE PERSONS OF THE TRINITY COVENANTED WITH EACH OTHER?

Some covenant theologians do not believe that there was a distinct covenant among the persons of the Trinity. They believe that the Covenant of Grace is the same thing as the covenant made before the creation of the world between the persons of the Trinity (we will discuss the differences between the two covenants later in this chapter). But there are good and solid, biblical reasons for believing that the Father covenanted with the Son and the Holy Spirit in order to accomplish the redemption of His people. That is why theologians call it the Covenant of Redemption, to distinguish it from the Covenant of Grace. Let's take a look.

1. John 6:37ff[28]: The Gospel of John records many occasions on which Jesus talks about His relationship with His Father, and why He (Jesus) came into the world. These explanations by Jesus form

---

[28] One of the most significant of the early covenant theologians, Caspar Olevianus (1536-1587), saw this as one of many passages that teach a pretemporal covenant between the persons of the Trinity. See page 63 of his Latin work, *De substantia foederis inter Deum et electos* (The Substance of the Covenant Between God and the Elect).

much of our understanding about the Covenant of Redemption. In John 6:37-40, Jesus says

> Everyone whom the Father gives to me will come to me; and the one who comes to me I will certainly never expel. For I came down from heaven not to do my own will, but to do instead the will of Him who sent me. And this is the will of Him who sent me: that I should lose none of all whom He has given to me; instead, I will raise him up on the last day. For this is the will of my Father, that everyone who beholds the Son and believes in Him may have eternal life; and I will raise him up on the last day.

These words of our Savior give us a glimpse into the relationship of the persons of the Trinity, and how they worked together for our salvation. The eternal Son of God did not volunteer to become incarnate; He was not a renegade who decided to go off on His own; and He was not elected by a majority vote of the Father and the Holy Spirit. Though all three persons of the Trinity are equal in power and glory, when it came to saving His lost people, the Father *sent* His Son. In fact, this passage even describes part of the reward that the Son would earn if He kept the covenant: "all whom [My Father] has given to me." One of the demands the Father made of His Son was that He should not lose any of His people. It was the Father's *will*—His covenantal command—that the Son actually and truly accomplish the salvation of every single human being whom the Father had given Him. If He kept this covenant, He would be rewarded with eternal fellowship with those elect (v. 39) in His Kingdom. However, if He did not accomplish their salvation, he would lose all of them.

This is simple justice. It is not mean, hateful or cruel. It does not make the Father any less of a Father, nor does it detract from His love for His Son. The Father has the right to determine what His Son's obedience is worth. He has the right to give His Son any reward that He wants to give Him for a job perfectly done. In this case, the reward is eternal fellowship with the elect.

In summary then, we have at least two essential elements of a covenant. First, God enforced the covenant. As the Lord of the covenant, the Father sent His servant—His own Son—to keep the covenant, and He also bestows the blessing of the covenant (His people) on the condition of doing His will. Second, there is the final outcome of the covenant: the blessing of dwelling eternally with His chosen people. So if we have the ingredients or "stuff" of a covenant, then we have a covenant.

2. John 10:15-30: This passage is very similar to John 6:37-40. But here, Jesus refers to Himself as 'the Good Shepherd' and to the elect as 'His sheep.' The idea is the same: the Father gives the sheep to Jesus. But He goes a bit farther than He did in the previous passage. In John 6 Jesus says that He will "lose none of all whom [the Father] has given" to Him. But in John 10:28 and 29, Jesus says that no one is able to snatch His sheep from His hand. Far from a sinful arrogance, Jesus is expressing the only possible outcome of the covenant for the eternal Son of God. It is true that Jesus is fully human and without sin (because sin is the result of the Fall, not the result of being human). But He is also fully God. Therefore, He could no more break the covenant (i.e., fail to save all of His sheep) than He could stop being God.

It is not possible for Jesus to talk about the certainty of the outcome, without implying the covenant between His Father and Himself. Besides, what would "the outcome" *mean*—what would it refer to—without the covenant? Again, since we have the stuff of a covenant—the sheep as the reward for Jesus' covenantal obedience— we have a covenant.

3. John 17: This passage records the High Priestly prayer of Jesus before His death on the cross. He repeats some of the same things from John chapters 6 and 10: the Father gave Him a people, and sent Him into the world to save those people. But there is an important difference here. In the opening verses of John chapter 17, Jesus addresses His Father as the obedient Son who has done what was required of Him, and therefore *deserves* the promised reward. He says

> I have glorified Thee on the earth by completing the work that Thou gavest me to do; now glorify Thou me, Father, with Thyself, with the glory I had with Thee before the world existed. (John 17:4, 5)

In His prayer, Jesus uses the principle found in Romans 4:4—"But to the one who works, his wages are not considered as grace, but as a debt owed." He is praying according to the principle of simple justice. It is as if He is saying to His Father, *"Father, You said that You would glorify Me if I did what You told Me to do. I have perfectly completed all the work that You sent Me to do. Now You owe it to Me to glorify Me."*

Some people recoil in shock and horror when they hear this analysis of Jesus' prayer. They say, that God does not, and never did, relate to his people on the basis of a works or merit principle.[29] If that were true, then Jesus' prayer would appear inappropriate at best. But the very fact that our Savior is able to address His Father that way suggests that justice—not grace—was the way in which He earned the reward of the covenant.

4. 1 Timothy 3:16: In the previous passages, we have seen that part of what the Father held out to His eternal Son as the reward for His obedience, was eternal fellowship with the elect. Obviously, for us who believe, the good news of the Gospel is that Jesus did accomplish our salvation. But 1 Timothy 3:16 gives us additional

---

[29] Shepherd, Norman. *The Call of Grace: How the Covenant Illuminates Salvation and Evangelism* (Phillipsburg: P&R Publishing, 2000), 61.

evidence that Jesus kept the covenant and earned the reward. The inspired apostle Paul says

> By common confession, the mystery of godliness is great:
> He who was revealed in the flesh,
> Justified by the Spirit,
> Beheld by angels,
> Preached among the Gentiles,
> Believed upon in the world,
> Taken up in glory.

The person about whom Paul is writing is obvious: he is talking about Jesus. The second line of this early confession provides the compelling evidence that Jesus kept the covenant with His Father. Paul says that Jesus was *justified* by the Spirit. But if Jesus was justified, doesn't that mean that He was a sinner in need of salvation like us? Not at all! Remember, justification is the legal declaration that someone is righteous. In Jesus' case, He actually *was* (and is) righteous. In our case, we are justified because *His* righteousness is imputed to us, or counted as our own.

But when was Jesus justified? Two clues will give us the answer. First, Romans 4:25 tells us that Jesus was *raised* for our justification. Second, if (eternal) death is the consequence of sin—and Jesus took our consequence of death upon Himself—then what would the consequence of perfect obedience be? The consequence would be *resurrection*—or eternal life in the New Creation. That is exactly what happened to Jesus. He *did* die, but not because *He* deserved to die. He died because *we* deserved to die. Because of His perfect obedience to His Father's covenant commands, Jesus deserved to *live*. So that is the reward that He received three days after His crucifixion. He was raised to New Life in the body of the New Creation. When Jesus was raised from the dead, He was justified by the Holy Spirit. His resurrection was God's way of publicly and legally declaring Jesus to be perfectly righteous. So if the resurrection was part of Christ's reward for obeying His Father perfectly, then that reward indicates that there was a covenant between the Heavenly Father and His eternal Son.

5. Luke 22:29 and 30: All of the Scriptures we have examined up to this point have supported the claim that the Father had entered into a covenant of works with His eternal Son. There is no Bible verse that spells it out in precise detail. But there doesn't have to be. The Bible teaches that God is a triunity—one God in three persons. Yet you will never find the word "Trinity" in your Bible. In the same way, the Bible teaches that from all eternity, there was a covenant of works between the Father and the Son. Yet when we try to find all of this in one verse, we come up short.

But is there a passage that at least uses the word "covenant" in describing the relationship between the Father and the Son? Yes, there is. If there is one passage that says it more clearly than any other, Luke 22:29-30 is it. Here Luke records an argument among the disciples about which of them was the greatest. Jesus—the second person of the Trinity who became a human being like us—stops their mouths by describing *Himself* as the humble servant of the Father. God in human flesh, who deserves to be bowed down to, worshiped and served, says that He came to serve *us*, not to be served Himself. Toward the end of His rebuke, Jesus said to His disciples,

> Since the Father has covenanted a Kingdom to Me, I also covenant [a Kingdom] to you so that you might eat and drink at My table in My Kingdom; and you will sit on thrones, judging the twelve tribes of Israel.

The Greek word for "covenant" is *diatheke* (dee-ah-thay-kay), and forms of *diatheke* are used twice in Luke 22:29. However all of the English translations use different words to translate *diatheke*. The *idea* of a covenant is still there in the English versions, even though they use words like, "grant," "confer," "appoint" and "bestow."[30]

It is also important to notice that Jesus now clearly includes the Kingdom as part of the reward of the covenant. Not only did Jesus merit eternal life for God's chosen people, but He merited the Kingdom for them as well. That is why we can say that if Jesus kept the covenant with His Father perfectly, He would earn eternal fellowship with the elect in the Kingdom of Heaven.

6. The Two Adams: In the last chapter, we appealed to the apostle Paul's theology of the two Adams to prove that the first Adam was related to God in terms of a covenant of works. So it may appear to be circular reasoning to turn right around and appeal to the two Adams to prove that the Last Adam was involved in a covenant of works with His Father. But this is not circular reasoning. First, the covenant of works with Adam and with Christ can be demonstrated and supported by other Scriptures. They do not rely solely on Romans 5, 1 Corinthians 15 and Ephesians 5. Second, when Paul contrasts the outcomes of Adam's and Christ's covenants in Romans 5, he proves that both of them were related to the Father on the basis of simple justice and the principle of works. If we ask how Adam and Christ arrived at their respective covenant outcomes, the answer for Adam would be his disobedience (Rom. 5:18a, 19a) and the answer for Christ would be his obedience (Rom. 5:18b, 19b). So Paul's theology of the two Adam's already contains evidence of covenants of works for both Adam and Christ.

We have already seen how Paul compares and contrasts Adam and Christ. He can compare them because they were both involved in a covenant of works with the Father where the eternal

---

[30] There are also some Old Testament passages that reveal God's covenant with the Son before the incarnation—even from eternity past. For example, see Psalm 89:3 and Isaiah 42:6. Psalm 110:4 does not use the term "covenant," but it describes God swearing an oath: the heart of a covenant.

reward was offered for their obedience and the eternal curse was threatened for their disobedience. He can contrast them because the first Adam broke the covenant of works and earned condemnation and Hell for all humanity; but the Last Adam kept the covenant of works and earned justification and eternal life in the Kingdom of God for the elect. But the comparisons or parallels become even more rich and beautiful in the Gospels.

For starters, the first Adam was put on probation in the Garden of Eden. The Tree of the Knowledge of Good and Evil was the probation—if he abstained from it, he would receive the covenant reward; but if he ate from it, he would certainly receive the covenant curse. In much the same way, the Last Adam was put on probation during His forty days in the wilderness. In fact, Matthew tells us that the purpose for the Spirit taking Christ to the desert was for Him to be tempted by the Devil.

But while the first Adam was in a garden before the Fall, the Last Adam found himself driven (Mark 1:12) out into a desert wilderness after the Fall. The Devil tempted the first Adam with the vain idea of trying to be God himself. But the Devil tempted the Last Adam with trading the suffering of the cross for recognizing him (the Devil) as Lord.

There are other passages that compare and contrast Adam and Christ (e.g., Eph. 5:22-33). But if other Scriptures refer to a covenant with Adam—and if the stuff of a covenant was present at creation with the threat of a curse and the offer of a reward—then the Last Adam was also covenantally related to the Father. Just as it was pointed out in the last chapter, it would make no sense to compare and contrast Adam and Christ if they were not both involved in the same kind of covenant. Only if Adam and Christ were both bound to the Father by a covenant of works would it make sense to contrast the sin, disobedience and condemnation of Adam with the righteousness, obedience and justification of Christ. Besides, we have seen the biblical evidence that Adam was to merit eternal life in the New Creation by keeping God's covenant. Even though Adam failed, the New Testament announces to us that the Last Adam has not only earned that eternal life in the New Creation, but He actually entered into it in His resurrection.

WHAT IS THE DIFFERENCE BETWEEN THE COVENANT OF REDEMPTION AND THE COVENANT OF GRACE?

As we stated earlier in this chapter, some covenant theologians do not believe that there was a distinct covenant between the Father and the Son. They believe that the covenant between the Father and the Son is the same as the Covenant of Grace. These theologians tend to look to Question 31 of the Westminster Larger Catechism to support their belief.[31] Even though we have not yet come to the Covenant of Grace in this book, we will examine the differences between the Covenant of Redemption and the Covenant of Grace, because nothing less than the Gospel is at stake.

The first difference between the Covenant of Grace and the Covenant of Redemption is the membership of each covenant. In the Covenant of Grace, not only people who claim to trust Christ, but their children also, are members of the covenant. That is why just as God dealt with entire households together in the Old Testament (Gen. 17) so He continues to deal with entire households together in the New Testament (John 4:53; Acts 11:14; 16:14, 15, 31-34; 18:8; 1 Cor. 1:16; 16:15; Phil. 4:22; 2 Tim. 4:19). The membership of the covenant of grace is not pure—some

---

[31] Question and Answer 31 of the Westminster Larger Catechism reads:
Q31: With whom was the covenant of grace made?
A31: The covenant of grace was made with Christ as the second Adam, and in him with all the elect as his seed. (Gal. 3:16; Rom. 5:15-21; Isa. 53:10-11)
However, many who subscribe the Westminster Standards as a faithful summary of biblical truth are quick to point out that if the "Covenant of Grace" is understood *not* in its historical administration, but in terms of the eternal plan of God, there is no problem with the catechism.

unbelievers are currently members, but will be cut off at the Last Day (Rom. 11:16-24) and some members fall away (Heb. 2:1-4; 6:4-6; 10:26-31). So it is possible to have believers and unbelievers as members of the Covenant of Grace.

On the other hand, the membership of the Covenant of Redemption *is* pure. If you revisit the passages in the Gospel of John that we examined earlier in the chapter, you will see that the Father did not give the Son any unbelievers as a reward. Only God's chosen people belong to the Covenant of Redemption.

So if we say that the Covenant of Grace and the Covenant of Redemption are the same covenant, then we distort the Gospel in terms of covenant membership. Obviously, membership cannot *include* certain unbelievers and *exclude* those same unbelievers at the same time and in the same relationship. So if we include certain unbelievers, then we must say that Christ accomplished the salvation of some people who will end up in Hell. That is not only contradictory, but it also slanders Christ. Yet if we exclude all unbelievers, then we must pretend to have God's knowledge of which persons are of the elect and which persons are not. But of course we don't share in God's knowledge, and so we run the very real risk of mistakenly excluding some true believers along with unbelievers.

If we accept the biblical distinction between the Covenant of Grace and the Covenant of Redemption, we avoid these problems altogether. We understand that from all eternity, God guaranteed the salvation of a definite number of people—as many as the number of stars in the sky (Gen. 15:5, 6; Rom. 4:16-24; Gal. 3:25-29). But we also understand that as the message of the Gospel goes out and people identify themselves with Christ and His people, some unbelievers will join the ranks (Acts 8:9-24; Heb. 10:26-31).

The second difference between the Covenant of Grace and the Covenant of Redemption is the relationship between the covenant Lord and the covenant servant. In the Covenant of Grace, Christ is the covenant Lord, and believers with their children are His covenant servants. The New Testament teaches this in various ways, but perhaps the clearest examples are the passages about Christ being the "Head" of His Church. When Paul calls Christ the Head of the Church he is not talking about body parts, but about the position of ultimate authority. Of course, another classic passage is Philippians 2:9-11, in which all honor and glory is given to Christ as the King, the Lord, by His creaturely subjects.

Yet in the Covenant of Redemption, the Father is the covenant Lord and Christ is His servant. Isaiah describes Christ as the "suffering servant" of Yahweh. As we saw earlier in Luke 22, Jesus tells His disciples that He came in order to serve God's people, not to be served by us. He even illustrated this by washing His disciples' feet.

In fact, Jesus Himself draws this distinction between the Lords of the two covenants and the servants of the two covenants in Luke 22:29 and 30. There He says that He received the Kingdom by means of a covenant with His Father. But He says that His disciples receive the Kingdom by means of a covenant with Himself (Jesus). Not only that, but Jesus argues for His covenant with us *based on* His Father's covenant with Himself—"*Since* the Father has covenanted a Kingdom to me, I *also* covenant a Kingdom to you..." (Luke 22:29, emphasis mine). Regardless of what some covenant theologians think, our Lord did not believe that the covenant with His Father is the same as His covenant with us.

The next difference between these two covenants shows up in the biblical concept of a covenant mediator. God, who is holy, cannot dwell with sinful creatures. His holiness would bring about our death. Yet He loves us in spite of our sin, and has provided a way for us to have fellowship with Him even while we are still sinners. He has provided His own Son as mediator. We do not just waltz into God's presence as if He were fortunate to have us. We come humbly before Him because of—and *only* because of Christ. Our Savior has made it possible for us to enter into God's holy presence by His sacrificial death and perfect obedience on our behalf. He also pleads our case before His Father as our Advocate (1 John 2:1). The author of Hebrews says that Christ is the mediator of a New and better covenant (Heb. 8:6). Jesus mediates the covenant between God and us so that we may pray to and worship Him safely and without fear.

But if the job of a covenant mediator is to make it safe for sinful creatures to approach God who is holy, then what about the Covenant of Redemption? Does the covenant between the Father and the Son require a mediator? No, it doesn't. That is exactly why Paul says, in Galatians 3:20, "Now a mediator does not mediate for just one party, but God is one." The biblical doctrine of the Trinity is a mystery: the Father and the Son are two distinct persons—yet they are one God. Paul's point is that mediators only mediate when there are two parties involved. But in the case of the trinity, there is only one party, and therefore there is no need for a mediator.[32]

The last and most important difference between the Covenant of Grace and the Covenant of Redemption is the difference between works and faith, justice and grace. Even though we deserve God's wrath, we are saved in spite of our sin (Eph. 2:5, 8; Rom. 3:24) apart from any of our own works (Rom. 3:28; 4:5; Gal. 2:16; 3:11, 12). God Himself provides everything that we lack, in order to ensure our eternal life with Him. As sinful creatures, we cannot survive the ultimate judgment of God's wrath. We need a second Adam who is a (sinless) creature and yet more than a creature—the God-man—who can bear our punishment in our place. As covenant breakers, we cannot provide God with the perfect obedience that He demands. We need the same God-man to obey

---

[32] I am completely indebted to Dr. Steven Baugh from Westminster Theological Seminary in California for this insight from and into Galatians 3:20. See his article "Galatians 3:20 and the Covenant of Redemption," *Westminster Theological Journal* 66, no. 1 (Spring 2004): 49-70.

for us—to please God for us—so that His obedience might be counted as our own obedience, and God might be pleased with us for *His* sake. God didn't have to do those things. The fair thing— the just thing—would have been for God to punish us for eternity. But in the Covenant of Grace, God gives us (free of charge to us) the blessing of New, eternal life with Him in His Kingdom.

Yet in the Covenant of Redemption, the blessing did not come free of charge to the Son. The Father offered Him eternal fellowship with the elect in the Kingdom *if He obeyed the Father's commands perfectly.* Knowing our own sin, we may wonder why the Father offered us as the *reward* of the covenant, rather than the curse. But God is the one who makes and enforces the covenants. He can arrange the covenants however it pleases Him. He can choose the reward, and He can choose what He wants His covenant servants to do to earn the reward. In the case of the Covenant of Redemption, the Father decreed that His Son's obedience was worth eternal life with us. Jesus obeyed His Father perfectly, and was able to demand the reward as a result. Though Jesus lived on earth as one of us, He was not sinful. He never needed His Father's help: He never needed forgiveness of sins and He never needed someone else to obey in His place. He did it Himself with no problem. Therefore, the Heavenly Father related to Jesus on the basis of justice and not grace.

We have seen before—but it always bears repeating—that justice-works and grace-faith are opposite principles when it comes to receiving the covenant blessing. Romans 4:4-5, 11:6 and Galatians 3:11, 12-18 all drive this point home. That is why it is a threat to the Gospel to say that the Covenant of Grace and the Covenant of Redemption are the same covenant. If we say that they are identical, then we run the risk of believing that the Father treated the eternal Son of God as a sinner who actually *deserved* punishment, but received blessing instead (grace). But we also run the risk of believing that God will bless us for *our* obedience and punish *us* for our disobedience (justice). This is the very reason why we cannot confuse the Lords and the servants of the two different covenants. In the Covenant of Grace, the Lord Christ treats us graciously, providing blessing in spite of our sin. In the Covenant of Redemption the Father is the Lord and He treats His servant Son justly or fairly on the basis of His Son's works.

CONCLUSION

Believe it or not, this eternal covenant between the persons of the Trinity is one of the most important covenants of all. Everything depended on the obedience of the first man Adam in the covenant of creation. But he dashed our hopes to pieces when he fell. Yet God was not going to let His chosen people spend eternity in Hell. He sent His only Son as the Last Adam, to accomplish what the first Adam failed to do. Once again, *everything* depends upon His obedience. In fact, this covenant of works between the Father and the Son forms the skeleton that supports all of the other covenants after the Fall. But how could that be? How could a covenant of works turn out to be, in a sense, more important than the Covenant of Grace?

Think of it this way. God offered to Adam eternal life in the Kingdom of the New Creation *if he obeyed perfectly.* However, God also threatened Adam with eternal death in Hell *if he disobeyed.* By covenantally binding Himself to Adam, God's justice was on the line. If Adam obeyed perfectly, God owed him the Heavenly reward He had held out. But if Adam disobeyed, God owed him the curse instead. Adam disobeyed. Yet God had chosen a people to live with Him forever. How could He give Adam–the first covenant representative of humanity–the justice he deserved (and that we deserve because of him), and still dwell with His people in Heaven? If He simply poured out His justice and wrath on Adam, effectively ending the human race, He wouldn't have a chosen people to enjoy eternally. That was not an option, since He had already decreed from all eternity to save the elect (Mt. 25:34; Eph. 1:4). On the other hand, if He overlooked Adam's sin, He would not be just or fair. If God simply "forgot about it," His threat from Genesis 2:17 would be meaningless; it would have no teeth; it would be laughable and able to be mocked. Besides, if God is not just, then God is not God (Gen. 18:25).

But God was not out of options. Instead of despising His justice, God upheld, recognized and sustained His justice. He sent His Son into the world as the Last Adam to both bear the just punishment that the first Adam (and we) deserved as well as to obey His law perfectly so that the elect could have His righteousness as their own. So when God graciously gives us blessings when we deserve punishment, it is only because He dealt fairly with His Son. In other words, what is for us a Covenant of Grace was for Christ, a covenant of works. God can graciously give us eternal life in His Kingdom because Christ merited life in that Kingdom by His perfect obedience. God can forgive our sins because Christ bore the curse that we deserved.

Even the covenant of common grace (that we will examine in the next chapter), depends upon the Covenant of Redemption between Father and Son. Both believers and unbelievers can continue to live and enjoy the blessings of this life because the Last Adam was legally bound to come into history and save the elect. But in order for the Last Adam to have human parents and to have the elect to save, life would have to go on—history would have to go on. Human life and history were allowed to continue for the sake of the coming of the Son of God.

If we deny the Covenant of Redemption we threaten the Gospel of justification by grace alone through faith alone because of Christ alone. We do this by eliminating the covenant of works of the Last Adam. The first man Adam had broken the original covenant of works in the Covenant of Creation. Once broken, it could not be reinstated. That is why there is *another* covenant of works for *another* Adam. Pretending that there was no eternal covenant of works between the Father and the Son leaves Christ in a position where He would be less than a perfect Redeemer. If the Mosaic covenant were Christ's covenant, then the geo-political land of Canaan would be all that He could merit for us (as we will see in chapter six). On the other hand, if the New Covenant were Christ's covenant, then the Father would be dealing with Him on the basis of grace—as if He were a sinner like you and me, *deserving* God's wrath and receiving the Kingdom *in spite of that* (as we will see in chapter seven). Neither option is biblical. Only an eternal covenant of works between the Father and the Son allows for the possibility of Christ meriting the blessings of our salvation for us.

Covenant *Before* Creation

4

Grace to Everyone and Everything: The Covenant of Common Grace

Grace to Everyone and Everything

Unfortunately, instead of keeping the covenant by abstaining from the Tree of the Knowledge of Good and Evil, doing the positive things that God required of him and earning the right to eat of the Tree of Life so that we could all enter into the ultimate Kingdom of God in the New Creation—instead of doing all of that, the first Adam violated the covenant of creation. He Fell.

Instead of cherishing his wife enough to keep her from this sin so that he could present her perfectly righteous before God (Eph. 5:25-27, 32), Adam left her to fend for herself. When the serpent came to her and challenged the authority of God's covenantal word—"Hath God said, 'You shall not eat of any tree of the garden?'"—where was Adam? The biblical text does not mention him, but he should have disputed the serpent's lie. God had not attached the threat of eternal Death to *every* tree in the garden, but only to one tree.

Instead of loving his wife, as he should have, so that he could present her without blame before God (Eph. 5:25-27, 32), Adam let her add to the serpent's distortion of God's word. It is true that she tried to refute the lie by explaining that God had not forbidden them to eat from *all* the trees. She explained that God had only forbidden them to eat from *and touch* the one tree (Gen. 3:2). But God had only said, "...from the Tree of the Knowledge of Good and Evil you shall not *eat*, for in the day that you *eat* from it you will certainly die." She had added her own rule to God's rule, and Adam should have corrected that.

Instead of giving himself up for his wife so that he could present her spotless and without blemish before God (Eph. 5:25-27, 32), Adam let her—and himself—think that they could be gods themselves, "knowing" good and evil. The serpent responded to Adam's wife: "You will not certainly die!" (Gen. 3:4). After all, the serpent reasoned, God was just a selfish tyrant who didn't want anyone else to have access to His powerful knowledge. So Adam and his wife believed this creature rather than their covenantal

Creator. By eating the fruit of the Tree of the Knowledge of Good and Evil, they were declaring that they knew what was good and what was evil better than God did. By eating the fruit of the Tree of the Knowledge of Good and Evil, the first man Adam failed to secure the covenant blessings for himself and the rest of humanity.

So Judgment Day came. It would have come either way—whether Adam had obeyed or disobeyed. Adam's works—whether good or bad—would have to be evaluated. The Almighty Judge would have to render a verdict: justified or condemned (Rom. 5:12-19).

And He did. But our English translations miss it because they mistranslate one of the Hebrew words. Genesis 3:8 should read, "Then they heard the sound of the LORD God striding in as the *Spirit* of the Day, and Adam and his wife hid from the face of the LORD God amongst the trees of the garden." (emphasis mine) The Hebrew word *ruach* can be translated either "Spirit" or "wind" (sometimes "breath"). Instead of translating *ruach* as Spirit (as it should be in this case), all of the English versions translate it as "wind"—"God was walking in the *wind of the day*." But wind seems out of place in the story. So they dial the forecast down a few notches so that God was strolling in the "evening breeze" or the "cool of the day." But that doesn't fit either, does it? Consider the context: Adam and his wife had just violated the covenant that God had made with them—they had committed the very violation that God had sworn to punish with eternal death, and so God... was strolling along in the cool, evening breeze. It just doesn't fit the context.

The sound that Adam and his wife heard was the sound of the Almighty Judge proceeding into His courtroom for the great and final Day of Judgment. The Spirit of the Day had arrived for the Great Day, the Final Day, the Day of Judgment. Genesis 3:8 is all about eschatology. The end had come, just as God said it would—

"In the day that you eat from it you will certainly die"—and here He was, to sentence to the two offenders.[33]

But the sentence that He delivered did not match the covenant curse of Genesis 2:17. It is true that he pronounced curses upon Adam, his wife, their descendants and the rest of creation. Adam's wife—and all future women—would experience terrible pain in childbirth (Gen. 3:16). Those same women would also desire to take over their husband's God-given office of "head of household." They would want to overthrow the marriage-government that God had established (Gen. 3:16). Plus, husbands would "lord it over" or tyrannize and oppress their wives (Gen. 3:16). By the same token, God cursed the ground so that the life-sustaining, family-supporting work that Adam (and all future men) would do would be hard, painful and frustrating (Gen. 3:17-19). Instead of entering the New Creation that Adam should have earned, all human beings—men and women alike—would return to the same dust of this earth from which God had created them (Gen. 3:19).

Certainly these curses sound painful and frightening. But what did Adam and his wife *deserve* according to the way God had arranged the covenant of creation? They deserved ultimate condemnation (Rom. 5:16, 18) and eternal death in Hell (Rom. 5:12, 15, 17). Yet the curses of Genesis 3:16-19 were not ultimate. The death spoken of as "returning to the dust of the ground" is death according to this creation, not the Death of eternal torment and punishment. According to God's threat against Adam and his wife in Genesis 2:17, we would have at least expected their hearts to stop cold, their lungs to cease breathing—or maybe we would have expected God to have completely removed the oxygen they breathed before sending them to Hell. That would seem to be the very least

---

[33] This account of Genesis 3:8 is based upon the exegesis of Meredith G. Kline in his book *Images of the Spirit*, (Eugene: Wipf and Stock Publishers, 1998), ch. 4. Cf. also his book *Kingdom Prologue*, (Overland Park: Two Age Press, 2000), 47-48, 128-130, 145, 205-206, 208-210, 218, 277.

that these rebels could suffer for their offenses against their good, holy, kind and just Creator.

Yet human life did not come to a sudden end in Genesis chapter 3. In fact, all of the curses in Genesis 3:16-19 imply that life would go on. Adam's wife would have to be alive in order to experience pain in childbirth. Not only that, but that curse also implies that children would continue to be born—humanity would live on. Husbands and wives could not have marriage problems unless they continued to live. Men had to be alive in order to struggle against the ground to provide for their families. It would seem, then, that the Great Judge of Heaven and earth had granted humanity a stay of execution. Somewhat like the state governor who delays the electrocution or lethal injection at the last minute, God had just proceeded into the courtroom to read His verdict and sentence the guilty, yet He had postponed the Final Judgment.

We don't just read this into Genesis 3. God provides His own interpretation for us in the New Testament.

> Or do you despise the riches of His grace and His patience, bearing with you, not understanding that the kindness of God is leading you to repentance? In accordance with your stubbornness and your unrepentant heart, you are storing up wrath for yourself on the Day of Wrath and revelation of the righteous judgment of God. (Rom. 2:4, 5)

> What if God, wanting to demonstrate wrath and make His power known, produced, with great patience, objects of wrath prepared for destruction? (Rom. 9:22)

> ...at the revelation of the Lord Jesus from Heaven with His powerful angels in flaming fire, inflicting punishment on those who do not know God and

who do not listen to the Gospel of our Lord Jesus. (2 Thess. 1:7-8)

If God had delivered His ultimate punishment to Adam and his wife in Genesis 3, the apostle Paul could not speak of God's patience, nor of God bearing with anyone. If God had sent Adam (and humanity) to Hell in Genesis 3, Paul could not talk about *storing up* wrath for the Day of Wrath that has not yet come and will not come until Christ returns.

What is God's attitude toward sinful humans from Genesis 3:8 up to the Last Day of Judgment? Again, the New Testament tells us:

> But the heavens and the earth that now are, are kept by the same word, reserved for fire on the Day of Judgment and destruction of wicked men... But the Lord is not slow to fulfill His promise as some consider slowness; instead He is patient with us, not wanting anyone to perish but [wanting] all to come to repentance. (2 Pet. 3:7, 9)

> For God loved the world in this way: that He gave His only begotten Son so that whoever believes on Him will not perish but have eternal life. For God did not send His Son into the world in order to condemn the world, but that through Him the world might be saved. (John 3:16, 17)

> Now then, we are ambassadors for Christ, as though God were pleading through us: we implore you on Christ's behalf, be reconciled to God. (2 Cor. 5:20, NKJV)

> ...this is good and pleasing in the sight of God our
> Savior who wants all men to be saved and to come to
> a knowledge of the truth. (1 Tim. 2:3, 4)

In spite of our offenses against Him personally and in Adam our first representative, God has a genuine love for us disgusting, sinful covenant breakers. He is being patient with us in order to save everyone whom He has chosen from the foundations of the world (Eph. 1:4)

So God graciously gave humanity the ability to go on living. But the life that Adam and his wife and you and I live on this earth is not eternal life in the ultimate Kingdom of God. Even though we deserve eternal death, God has given life to those who are His people *and* to those who are *not* His people. So this earthly life is a gift of grace because it is a blessing in spite of what we deserve, but it is not *saving* grace. It is grace that has provided earthly life for the first Adam's son Cain (and his descendants in unbelief) as well as his son Seth (and his descendants in the faith). It is grace that is *common* to believer and unbeliever alike. Hence, we call it "common grace."

It is absolutely vital that we understand what this means: there is a clear distinction between things holy and things common. Holy things (like the Church) are destined for the Heavenly Kingdom of God. Before the Fall, *everything* was holy and destined for the New Creation. But since the Fall, the Church is the holy alien in a common world. Common things (like culture) are destined to come to an end when God's stay of execution is up— when the *ultimate* and *final* Judgment Day arrives. But that does not make common things *bad* or *unholy*. After all, God ordained human culture to continue on after the fall. So culture is *good*—but it is not *holy* because it will not find its completion in the New Creation.

Yet in spite of His demerited favor, it was not long before one of God's human creatures took advantage of His common grace. When God was pleased with Abel's sacrifice and not Cain's, Cain murdered Abel in a jealous rage. So God cursed Cain for what he had done. He said,

> And now you are cursed from the ground, which has opened its mouth to receive your brother's blood from your hand. When you till the ground, it will no longer yield to you its strength; you will be a fugitive and a wanderer on the earth. (Gen. 4:11, 12, NRSV)

But Cain was afraid. He reasoned that a world in which God had turned away His face (Gen. 4:14) would be a horrifying place of anarchy and lawlessness. As a fugitive and a wanderer, Cain did not want to be murdered by the next person he met. Yet God rebuked Cain for his fear:

> But the LORD said to him, "Not so! Whoever kills Cain will undergo vengeance seven-fold." Thus the LORD gave an oath to Cain so that anyone who found him would not kill him. (Gen. 4:15)

Most of our English translations say that God "put a mark" on Cain—and so we tend to think of Cain as somehow looking different because of the "mark." But the Hebrew word ot (pronounced "oat") can also mean "a pledge" or "an assurance"—an oath—which is exactly what the context of the verse is about. God assured Cain that life on earth would not be lawless. In fact, this is where God began human government. God instituted the State by His oath to Cain that murder would be appropriately avenged.[34]

---

[34] This account of Genesis 4:15 is taken from the exegesis of Meredith G. Kline in "The Oracular Origin of the State," *Biblical and Near Eastern Studies*, ed. G.A. Tuttle, (Grand Rapids: Eerdmans, 1978), 132-141. Cf. also his *Kingdom Prologue*, (Overland Park: Two Age Press, 2000), 155, 164-165.

But just as human life on earth after the Fall is not the eternal life of the New Creation, so the institution of the State is not the Kingdom of God. Just as culture after the Fall is not holy—yet it is good because God decreed that it should continue—so the State is not holy. Yet at the same time, the State is also good because God established it. God had provided for a measure of justice on earth, but the State does not administer the ultimate justice of Judgment Day. In fact, as we will see later in this chapter, the State will come to an end at Judgment Day.

That is because the purpose of the State is not to do holy work. The purpose of the State is to do common work—work that is common to believers and unbelievers. God's job description for the State is not to enforce His holy commandments upon everyone everywhere. Instead, God intends the State to provide a stable environment for human life. After all, God had declared that human life would go on after Adam and Eve fell, and in Genesis 4:15 God provided an instrument of life-support.

As an institution of common grace, then, the State governs all people no matter what they believe. As Christians, we are commanded to obey the State (Rom. 13:1-7). Therefore, for us, all crimes are sins (unless, of course, the "crime" is obeying God's Word). But for the State, not all sins are crimes. The institution that God established in Genesis 4:15 did not have the mandate to punish anyone who didn't worship the triune God of Scripture, who worshipped images (or used images in religious worship), who took the name of the triune God in vain, who failed to keep the Sabbath, who was sexually impure—and the list could go on and on. The State is not the administrator of the Kingdom of God. Instead, it is God's instrument for both restraining humanity from being as bad as it could possibly be, as well as for relieving or lessening the effects of the common curse.

So with God's oath that there would be an institution to protect him from murder and mayhem (or to at least punish such criminals), Cain began to wander east of Eden where he began his family. Adam's family tree would have two main branches: the branch of believers (Seth) and the branch of unbelievers (Cain). Genesis 4:16-24 records the development of Cain's family, while Genesis 5 records the development of Seth's family. This family tree finds its ultimate significance in the second Adam, Jesus Christ who is the champion of all of Seth's true descendants.

Just as with culture and the State, it is important to understand that the institution of the family is something that believers and unbelievers have in common. The family is not holy. Otherwise, Cain and his descendants—in fact, every single human being—would be holy because everybody comes from a family (in some way, shape or form). Instead, the family is common—another institution of common grace. But unlike the State, which God established after the Fall, the family is part of creation itself. Adam and his wife were not created as "rugged individualists" who just happened to end up together. God created them with the identities of husband and wife, designed to produce children who would in turn, grow up into those identities themselves. As we will see later in the book, the family is vitally important to the covenants that are directly involved with our salvation. God uses the family in His covenantal salvation of His people. But just as the rest of the creation became common after the Fall, so did the institution of the family.

Yet the changed status of the family is not the only thing worth noticing in Genesis 4:16-24. Cain and his children began doing very important things. Cain built a city (4:17). Jabal developed the financial world of the ancient near east with its symbol of wealth: livestock (4:20). Jubal developed musical instruments (4:21). Tubal-Cain became the first blacksmith, making useful tools out of metal (4:22). The Bible does not condemn these cultural activities and artifacts. It simply reports them. The significance of these reports is that culture does not need to be

made holy (or made to *appear* to be holy) in order for it to be good
or for believers to enjoy it and participate in it.

God did not establish "secular" culture in Genesis 4 and
"Christian" culture in Genesis 5. As Michael Horton puts it in his
book *Putting Amazing Back Into Grace*, God has never organized any
"Christian concerts," produced any "Christian T-shirts" nor
promoted any "Christian businesses." Music, fashion and business
are good just the way they are. Those things are not set apart (holy),
*we—believers—*are. So believers and unbelievers can work together to
build cities, make money, make music and musical instruments, and
forge tools and other things out of metal. The difference comes (or
ought to come) in how we do our work. It is not the shoe that is
holy, but the shoemaker who has set apart Christ as Lord in his
heart, and makes each shoe as though God Himself had
commissioned him to make it.

THE NOAHIC COVENANT AND COMMON GRACE

There are actually two covenants involved in the story of
Noah. The first one was a unique covenant that the LORD made
with Noah and his family in Genesis 6 and 7 in order to save them
from the floodwaters that were so much like the Final Judgment.
For our purposes in this chapter, we will not be focusing on that
covenant. The other covenant, found in Genesis 8:20-9:17, is a
covenant that God made with all of creation. And yet this covenant
was not brand new. In Genesis 9:9-17, God said that He was
"confirming" or "maintaining" His covenant with all of creation—
including *all* of mankind. In other words, God's grace, that was
common to all creatures, as well as both believers and unbelievers—
God's common grace was covenantal ever since the Fall. The
Hebrew word that would have been used to say that God *made* a
covenant with creation (for the very first time) is *carat*. Yet instead
of *carat*, Genesis 9:9-17 says that God *haqym*—"confirmed" or
"maintained"—His covenant with all that He had made.

We all know the story well. God was displeased with humanity because of its sin. He was going to destroy every last person on the face of the earth—except Noah and his family. So He gave Noah detailed instructions to prepare an Ark to protect him and his family and pairs of all kinds of animals from the deadly floodwaters. Noah did as he was told. It rained for forty days and forty nights. Everyone outside the Ark died, but Noah and his family floated over the deep and darkness of the watery grave—just like everyone outside of Christ will be eternally condemned at the Final Judgment, but everyone who belongs to Christ has already been judged in His death on the cross (1 Peter 3:20, 21).

It was very much like the creation story all over again. In Genesis 1:2, the earth was formless and void; in Genesis 7:17-24 the flood again made the earth formless and void. In Genesis 1:2, the Spirit of God hovered over the face of the waters; in Genesis 8:1, God caused a wind (*ruach*—same word for "Spirit") to pass over the earth. What makes Noah's story different from creation is that in Genesis 6 through 9 God was starting over. Creation had to be destroyed and begun again. In that sense, Noah's story is like the Last Day. The apostle Peter describes this in terms of "the world that then was" which was destroyed by the flood (2 Peter 3:6) and "the heavens and earth that now are," which are reserved for fire on the Day of Judgment (2 Peter 3:7). Based on those two worlds of Noah's flood, Peter describes the time when this creation will be destroyed and the New Creation will be clothed upon it (2 Peter 3:10-13).

So as Noah and his family left the Ark, it was as if they were entering into a new creation (even though they were still sinful). One of the first things that Noah did was offer a burnt offering to the LORD. As the aroma of the offering ascended, God swore to Noah:

Never again shall I curse the ground for the sake of
man, though the imagination of the heart of man is

> evil from his earliest days; and never again shall I destroy every living thing as I have [just] done. For all the days of the earth: the season of sowing and harvest-time, cold and heat, summer and winter, day and night will not cease. (Gen. 8:21, 22)

God re-confirmed what he had sworn to Adam and Eve after the Fall: this creation (human life and all) would continue on until the Final Day of Judgment. In fact, this time, God attached a sign to the covenant—a rainbow—to remind us of His solemn oath not to destroy the earth by flood, but to preserve and sustain it until His appointed Last Day (Gen. 9:11-17). However, the rainbow was not given to believers only. God gave the sign of the covenant of common grace to all of creation. So all human beings can take comfort in the gracious promise of the rainbow.

But unlike the covenant of creation that depended upon Adam's obedience for the reward, God made the covenant of common grace—He promised to give the reward—*because of* Adam's sin (and humanity's sin). God's justice required Him to execute final judgment against Adam and his fellow human beings, according to the covenant of creation. But God's thoughts are higher than our thoughts and His ways are not our ways. In order to delay His final judgment, God would sustain this creation in the meantime.

CONCLUSION

What Adam and Eve deserved (and what we deserve) because of the Fall (and because of our own, personal sin) is eternal death in Hell, separated from the face of God. Yet in His wisdom, God postponed that ultimate sentence. As we saw in chapter 3, He postponed His ultimate judgment for the sake of Christ's death on the cross. That sacrificial death by the God-man would satisfy God's wrath against your sin and my sin. But if humanity did not continue on, the Last Adam would not be able to come into this world—for He would be born "of the seed of the woman" (Gen. 3:15, Rom. 1:3; Gal. 4:4). In that sense, then, Christ's death is the basis for God's covenant of common grace. To put it differently, the covenant of common grace is not *directly* related to our justification—but without common grace, there would be no humanity to justify and there would be no world for the Last Adam to enter so that He could merit our justification. So if we deny the covenant of common grace, then there is no good reason why the world continues to exist, and God could justly destroy all of creation before our salvation is consummated.

We all experience some sort of suffering, hardship or heartache in our lives in this world—some worse than others. But no matter what kind of suffering we go through—whether sickness, abandonment, rape, physical torture or murder—we must always remember that it simply cannot compare to what our sin truly deserves: eternity in Hell. This doesn't just apply to "all those unbelievers *out there*." You and I deserve to rot in Hell, too. Thankfully, Christ has borne that ultimate punishment for us who believe, so that we do not have to bear it ourselves. But that is not because of anything good in us, but only because God is gracious.

Yet in showing this *non-saving* grace to humanity, God was not favoring believers. "For He [the Father] causes the sun to rise on the evil and the good and He causes the rain to fall on the righteous as well as the wicked" (Mat. 5:45). This grace that ensures that life will go on (though we deserve to die) is *common* to believer *and* unbeliever. That means that this life can be enjoyed *with* unbelievers. We do not have to have a separate, parallel existence as Christians in order for our lives (i.e., this life) to be legitimate.

At the same time, that does not mean that either *everything* is common or that *everything* is holy. Since the Fall, the Church and her mission are the only things that are holy. Human culture, the family and the institution of the State are common (***not*** unholy nor wicked). As a result, God's covenant of common grace is far more relevant than we might think.

First, we do not have to create our own "Christian" version of cultural artifacts in order for those cultural artifacts to be good, legitimate or acceptable. The main reason for this is that according to the Bible, culture is neither "Christian" nor "non-Christian." Culture is one of the means that God uses for maintaining a stable environment in which to do His work of redemption. To pick just one example, we do not have to have "Christian music" (or "Christian rock") as opposed to "secular music" (or regular rock music).[35] For one thing, a guitar string plucked by a non-Christian is no different than a guitar string plucked by a Christian. If there is a difference, it is in heart of the person playing the music. But besides that, it is sadly the case that most non-Christian musicians are more *honest* in the content of their lyrics than most Christian musicians. While pop-Christianity is so busy *celebrating* everything, non-Christians seem to realize that death is sad and should be cried about; injustice is maddening and should be yelled about; hypocrisy is disgusting and should be rejected. Though non-Christians often come to wrong conclusions about things because they reject God's

---

[35] I would even go so far as to say that *popular culture* (rock music, television, modern radio, non-academic magazines, billboards, etc.) is actually *dangerous* if it is used as the type of media through which we communicate the gospel message. To try to communicate a message as life-or-death important as the gospel by means of entertainment media ends up trivializing and, indeed, mocking the very truth we want the world to receive. For a more complete treatment of this, read Kenneth Myers' book *All God's Children and Blue Suede Shoes: Christians and Popular Culture*. It seems to me that he still promotes the concept of "Christian culture" to some degree, but his is a far more thoughtful approach to cultural participation and interaction than most others. I also highly recommend two books by Neil Postman: *Amusing Ourselves to Death: Public Discourse in the Age of Television* and *Technopoly: The Surrender of Culture to Technology*. Postman is not a Christian, but his insights into how messages are shaped and even changed by the media through which they are communicated are so important that the Church cannot afford to ignore him.

interpretation of Himself and His creation, we would do well to join them in good, honest, cultural activity.

Second, the institution of the State is not a man-made institution that should be used as a tool for power plays and (illegitimately) controlling others. Instead, God instituted the State for the purpose of restraining humanity's wickedness, as well as for the purpose of lessening the effects of the common curse (i.e., the frustrating work, sickness, pain in childbirth and marital discord that afflicts believers and unbelievers alike).[36] That means that if we are to think biblically, we must rid the American church of any *identification* with any and all political parties. The Church is the membership of the Kingdom of God. The State is the membership of the kingdoms of this world. While unbelievers are only members of the kingdoms of this world, Christians are in a unique position of having "one foot in each world," so to speak. While we are on earth, we are members of both the kingdoms of this world, and the Kingdom of God. However, the Bible neither commands nor forbids membership in or identification with any political party. Therefore, individual Christians are free to join any political party according to his or her conscience. But we must always keep in mind that America is not unique in its relationship to God. Every other nation on earth is related to God in the same way that America is: by His *common* grace. America may provide freedoms that we greatly enjoy, but God did not make a covenant with America. And if God did not make a covenant with America, then He is not bound to us any differently than He is bound to every tribe and nation and tongue because of Genesis 8:22-9:1.

---

[36] The common grace institutions of the State and the family can be instruments of the common curse at the same time because of sin. The State may rightly punish murderers according to its mandate in Genesis 4:15, but it wrongly murders people when it wages aggressive war (rather than defensive war). Similarly, families rightly care for each member by God's design, but they can be instruments of abuse at the same time.

Finally, we should not buy into the ever-so-subtle notions that the universe has always existed and will always exist, or that the universe is the ultimate foundation that is necessary for the existence of everything else. The fact that laws of science do not change, the fact that the sun rises every morning, the fact that nature behaves the same way consistently—these facts are not *just* facts. The future will be like the past not only because God created the universe, but also because He entered into covenant with it. Though He should have destroyed His creation according to His justice because of the Fall, God made a covenant of common grace with creation. That covenant is why the future will be like the past. That covenant is why the sun rises every morning. The covenant of common grace is why scientific experiments can be repeated (because the laws of science and nature do not change).

So if we were to return to our diagram from chapter 2...

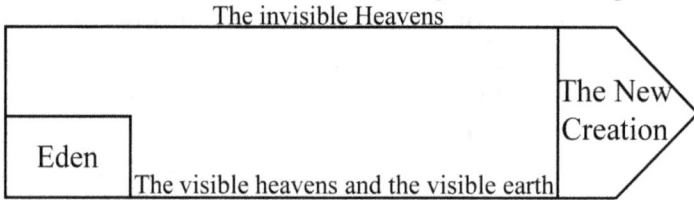
The invisible Heavens / Eden / The visible heavens and the visible earth / The New Creation

it would now look like this: Even though the first Adam was supposed to have earned eternal life in the ultimate Kingdom of God for us, He fell. From a human perspective, the Fall destroyed God's plan for dwelling with His human creatures in Heaven...

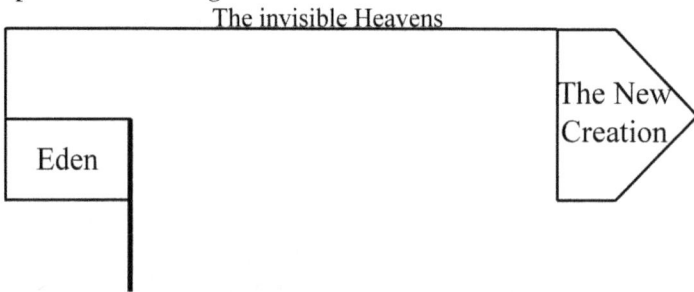
The invisible Heavens / Eden / The New Creation

But, of course the Fall did **not** destroy God's plan. Somehow, it was part of His plan all along. In fact, in spite of the Fall, God made the covenant of common grace with all of creation including all human beings (believers and unbelievers). By the covenant of common grace, God provided a stable environment in which the Last Adam would enter to accomplish the salvation of His people.

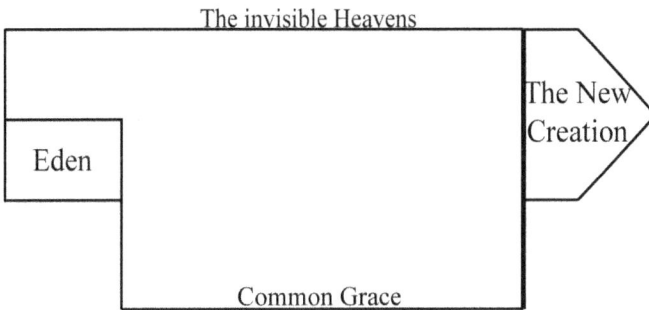

But creation will not continue on like this eternally. Though we will see in the next chapter that the covenant of grace *consummates* (or reaches its fulfillment and completion), the covenant of common grace *terminates*—it ends at the Final Judgment. Therefore, on the Last Day, human culture, the institution of the State and the institution of the family will come to an end and unbelievers will go to Hell.

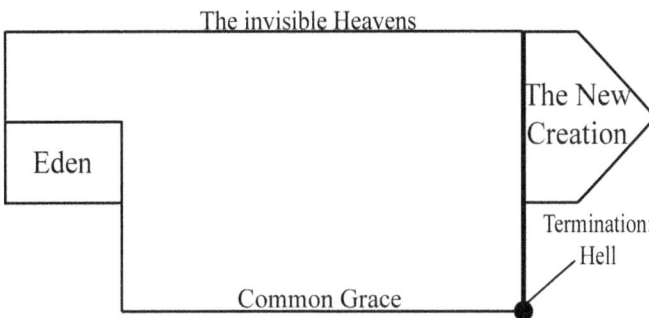

Sadly, many Christians want to see the institutions of common grace subjected to the Law of God *right now*. Of course we all long for the day when we (and everyone around us) live perfectly holy lives. But that longing is the longing for the Consummation. It is the longing for the arrival of the Final Judgment (that the Last Adam has borne for us) as well as the ultimate Kingdom of God. By desiring to see culture, the State and the family become holy institutions *now*, these Christians want the Consummation to arrive *before* God's appointed time. Their desire would amount to an indirect attack on the Gospel, because it would mean cutting short the time God has allotted for gathering His people. It would mean that Christ would lose some of those whom the Father had given him (Jn. 6:39). The meritorious obedience of the Last Adam would not be imputed to everyone whom the Father had intended.

Fortunately, God cannot violate his own oath. He has sworn that non-holy (common) things like seasons and harvests will continue "while the earth remains." The earth will come to an end in God's timing, not ours.

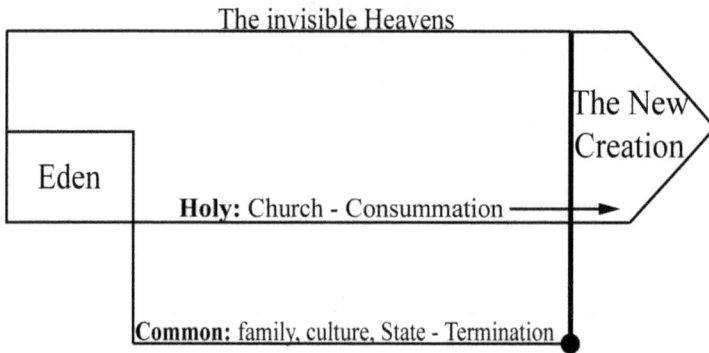

The invisible Heavens

Eden

The New Creation

Holy: Church - Consummation

Common: family, culture, State - Termination

In God's wisdom, there is a clear distinction between things that are holy and things that are common. Only the Church is holy, while culture, the State and the institution of the family are common to believer and unbeliever. Holy things and common things are never integrated or combined except when the Kingdom of God is present. We will see that more clearly in later chapters, but for now the holy and the common must never be confused.

5

The Covenant of Grace: From Genesis 3:15 to Abraham to the Last Day

The Covenant of Grace

In the covenant of common grace, God granted humanity a stay of execution when He stormed into His courtroom to sentence the guilty. That grace was common to all of creation, not just to human beings—and not just to believers. Yet in the middle of the list of common blessings and curses of Genesis 3 is the gem of the Gospel: "I will place hatred between you and the woman and [I will place hatred] between your descendants and her descendants. And He shall bruise your head, and you shall bruise His heel" (Gen. 3:15). For reasons that we may never understand, God loved us in spite of our sin and determined to save us from His own wrath in Hell. He announced the way in which He would ensure that we would still be able to live eternally with Him in Heaven.

You see, since Adam was our first covenant representative, we were all doomed when **he Fell**. Though we contribute our own sin on a daily basis, Adam's sin alone was enough to make us guilty, condemned and totally unable to dwell with God. Now that human nature is sinful because of the Fall, **we cannot please God ourselves**. We cannot please God ourselves because everything we do is stained and tainted by sin. In order for God to be pleased with us, **Somebody else must please Him *for* us**—not help us to first become pleasing to God[37]—not help us "to become the covenant keepers that God intended us to be from the beginning."[38] Somebody outside of ourselves must please God *in our place*—keep God's covenant *for* us. Somebody else must earn the ability for us to have the life of the New Creation in the ultimate Kingdom of God.

---

[37] This is the official position of the Roman Catholic Church as articulated in the Council of Trent in the Sixth Session, chapters 3, 5, 6, 7, 10, 16; Canons I, II, III, IV, VII, IX, XI, XII, XXI, XXIV, XXV, XXVI, XXVII, XXIX, XXXI. See *The Canons and Decrees of the Council of Trent*. (Rockford: TAN Books and Publishers, 1978). As of the writing of this book, the entire text of the Council of Trent may be found at http://history.hanover.edu/early/trent.htm.

[38] Shepherd, Norman. *The Call of Grace: How the Covenant Illuminates Salvation and Evangelism* (Phillipsburg: P&R Publishing, 2000), 57.

In Genesis 3:15, God not only set His people apart from the rest of humanity, but He also promised a Savior—another Adam who would succeed at keeping the covenant of works. According to God's sovereign promise, Eve would have a Son who would ultimately defeat the serpent. This Son would prevail where Adam had failed. But Eve's Son would achieve His victory in a way that we might consider foolish. Her Son would bruise the head of the serpent only *after* the serpent had bruised His heel. Though "bruising the head" and "bruising the heel" sound like minor injuries that can be healed quickly, they are figures of speech to describe death, destruction and defeat. So this hero-Son of Eve's would suffer *first*, before the reaching the glory of His victory. **He would win by losing.**

The New Testament interprets this One who suffered first and then entered into His glory as none other than Jesus Christ. First Peter 1:10-11 says that the Holy Spirit has been testifying not only in Genesis 3:15, but to the Old Testament prophets as well—testifying about Christ. God gives us His love and His favor because Christ is the descendant of Eve's who would defeat the devil for us by His death and resurrection. In Luke 24:25-27, Jesus identifies Himself as Eve's Son. He tells His disciples that His death and resurrection were necessary to fulfill what the Scriptures said about Him—that He would have to suffer first and then enter His glory.[39]

---

[39] Rev. Dr. Lee Irons also makes this connection in a sermon on the book of Job entitled "Suffering and the Triumph of God." Job's story is Christ's story. In Job's story, God "picks the fight" with Satan (Job 1:8), offering Job as His champion. Of course, we know what happens: Satan destroys everything except Job's wife and his own life. But it was God's plan all along to defeat Satan by Job's suffering—and God blessed him twice as much at the end of the story than He had at the beginning. The same is true of Christ in Genesis 3:15. Again, God picks the fight with Satan, this time offering His own Son as the champion. And again, it was God's plan all along to defeat Satan by Christ's suffering first—and only *after* suffering, to receive His glory.

So Genesis 3:15 is the Gospel in "seed" form. Seeds contain all the information that is necessary for the growth of a tree. Everything about a mature, full-grown, fruit-bearing tree is already contained in the seed. The Gospel of God's grace in Jesus Christ is very similar. Everything that the New Testament teaches us about the salvation that Christ has accomplished for us is already contained in Genesis 3:15. There are many details about our Savior that are not given there. But we know that He will be a man who will die. Yet we also know that He will live again because He defeats the devil after His own "defeat." As God does more redemptive deeds in history, the seed grows and blossoms as He reveals that Eve's Son will also be the Son of Abraham (Gen. 22:18; Acts 3:25-26; Gal. 3:16). Later, the seed grows into a sapling as God reveals that this New Adam will be the Son of David (2 Sam. 7:12ff; Acts 2:29-36)–the "stump of Jesse" (Isa. 11:1ff; Rom. 15:8-12). We even learn that this descendant of Eve's is also God Himself (John 10:30). Once Jesus arrives on the scene of history and accomplishes what He came to do, the tree is full-grown with flowers and fruit. He not only explains that He is Eve's Son, but He achieves everything promised in Genesis 3:15. Luke even traces His genealogy all the way back to Adam and Eve (Lk. 3:23-38).

But before we get too far ahead of ourselves, let's return to Genesis 3:15 to see how the seed begins to grow. After Adam and Eve were expelled from the Garden of Eden, the Bible tells us that Eve gave birth to a son whom she named Cain. Later, she had another son whom she named Abel. No doubt she hoped that one of her boys would be the champion God had promised. Sadly, neither son would bear that title because one day Cain murdered Abel out in a field. Cain was jealous that God had accepted Abel's animal sacrifice while He was displeased with Cain's crops. Instead of repenting of his sin, Cain was more worried about being murdered by the next person he met. So Cain showed himself to be the first unbeliever in human history, and Genesis 4:16-24 records the line of Cain's unbelieving descendants.

However, immediately after Cain's genealogy, the Bible tells us that Adam and Eve had a third son whom they named Seth. Genesis 4:26 says, "And Seth also bore a son, and he called his name Enosh. Then men began to be identified by the name of the Lord." So Seth's family and their descendants were believers in the second Adam, and Genesis chapter 5 records their genealogy.

From Genesis 3:15, then, two family trees begin. One family tree has the serpent, the Devil, as its father. The other family tree can trace its roots back to Eve as people of this earth. But more than that, they call themselves by the name of their Heavenly Father. They are the people of Jehovah, Yahweh's children. This last group of people participates in two worlds. As fallen creatures of this creation, they lived in tents as wandering cattle herders, played musical instruments and forged metal tools with Cain's children (Gen. 4:16-24). But as people who believed God's promise in Genesis 3:15, they were destined to live forever with God in the New Creation—and so they took their Father's name as their own.

Genesis 5 traces God's special, covenant people from Adam and Seth all the way down to Noah and his three sons Shem, Ham and Japheth. But Noah and his family mark the point in the history of God's covenants when God destroyed the world that then was with floodwater (2 Pet. 3:6). In the last chapter we saw how the flood was like both the original creation as well as the Final Judgment. In fact, in 2 Peter 3:6-7, Peter compares "the world that then was" (before the flood) with this creation, and he compares "the world that now is" (after the flood) with the New Creation. It was as if the flood was Noah's passing from this creation into the New Creation. Noah made it through the flood in the Ark. But Peter tells us that we survive the floodwaters of Final Judgment through the waters of baptism into Christ's death and resurrection (1 Pet. 3:20-21; cf. Rom. 6:1-14). In other words, what Peter means to say is that only Christ—the ultimate Adam—can safely carry sinners through God's wrath, whether Adam (after the Fall) or Noah or you or me.

So when Noah and his family left the Ark, they were starting the human race all over again. But it soon became clear that the world after the flood was only a *type* of the New Creation (i.e., an earthly picture of that future reality). Sin was not destroyed. As God would have it, Ham turned out to be from Cain's family, while Noah, Shem and Japheth were descendants of Seth. Ham sinned against Noah by exposing his nakedness. It is no accident that Satan did the same thing to Adam and Eve. Therefore, Noah's curse in Genesis 9:25-27 sounds quite similar to God's curse against the serpent in Genesis 3:15. God put hatred and war between the descendants of the serpent and the descendants of the woman. Noah announced conflict between Ham's children and the children of Shem and Japheth by making Ham's family the "servant of servants," slaves to his brothers (Gen. 9:25).

Ham's descendants are described in Genesis 10:6-20. Japheth's descendants are briefly listed in Genesis 10:2-5, and Shem's family tree is traced in Genesis 10:21-32 and 11:10-32. In fact, Shem's genealogy is traced all the way down to Abram. As we well know, Abram would become the father of the nation of Israel, the chosen people of God. From here on out, Scripture stops tracing the genealogy of the descendants of the serpent. Once we get to Abram, the main concern of the Bible is the people whom God is saving in the Covenant of Grace. Now we see that Eve's son who was prophesied in Genesis 3:15, would come from the family of Shem.

The heart of God's covenant with Abraham appears in Genesis chapter 15 where an amazing ceremony took place. There God sovereignly promised Abram that he would have an heir and a vast number of descendants. God required Abram to bring Him a three year-old heifer, a three year-old female goat, a three year-old ram, a turtledove and a pigeon. Then Abram was to cut them into two pieces (except the birds) and place them so that there was a row or a pathway between all the bloody animal halves. God put Abram into a deep sleep and He solemnly vowed to provide a land for his descendants (even though they would spend most of their lives as strangers and foreigners).

But then God appeared to Abram in the form of a smoking oven and a burning torch, and He made His way through the pieces of butchered animals on the path between them. By this, God showed Abram that He was deadly serious about this covenant. It was as if He were saying to Abram, "*If I do not keep the promises I have made to you, may what has happened to these animals, happen to Me—may I be put to death if I do not keep this covenant with you.*" God Himself would walk down into the valley of the shadow of death—if He broke His own covenant.

Yet ironically, God did undergo the curse of this covenant in the person of the Son when Christ died upon the cross. He had not broken His covenant with Abraham (nor any covenant for that matter), because God cannot lie (Heb. 6:13-18; Titus 1:2). Therefore, the oath that He swore to Abraham *guaranteed* the outcome of the covenant—it could not have happened any other way. Still, even though God had not broken the covenant, it was only by being Himself cursed by the punishment of Genesis 3:15 and 15:17 that He could keep His oath to Abraham.

Why was this the only way the covenant could be kept? Because God did not stop being just and fair. In fact, it is precisely *because* God is just, that He had to bear the curse in the person of the Son. God's justice *must* be satisfied. Abraham couldn't satisfy God's justice because he—along with all of Adam's children—was fallen. Therefore, in order for God's justice to be satisfied *and* for Abraham to live with God eternally, the Lord would have to bear the punishment that His own justice demanded. That is why Christ's heel was "bruised." The second Adam had to travel the pathway (Gen. 15:17) of a bloody death in order to save us; and by doing that, He became *the way* (John 14:6). What was for Abraham—and for us—a covenant of grace, *had* to be for Christ, a covenant of works. Yet even though He kept the covenant with His

Father perfectly and deserved the life of the New Creation, He was punished so that we would not have to be punished.

But God gave Abraham other promises besides numerous descendants. In the broader context of Genesis 12 through 18 and beyond, God also promised Abraham a land and a King. All three of these promises—the people, the land and the King—have been fulfilled. Obviously, the Jews descended from Abraham and are part of God's promise. But the apostle Paul tells us that Christ is the ultimate and true descendant of Abraham's (Gal. 3:16)—and we are Abraham's promised descendants because we belong to Christ (Gal. 3:29; cf. Rom. 4:16; 9:7ff; 11:16-24). In Genesis 12:1, God promised Abraham a land for himself and his descendants to dwell in. As the biblical story of God's Kingdom and covenants goes on, we discover that the land of Canaan is part of God's promise (Joshua 24). But the author of the book of Hebrews tells us that the ultimate and true land that God promised to Abraham and his descendants is Heaven itself (Heb. 11:8-16; esp. vv. 15-16). But God also promised Abraham a King (Gen. 17:6, 16). King David of Israel is part of that promise (Mt. 1:1). But the ultimate and true King whom God had promised Abraham is our Lord Jesus Christ (Mt. 1:1; Lk. 1:32-33, 69-73).

So once again, eschatology is present even in the earliest stages of the Covenant of Grace—in Genesis 3:15, in Noah's flood and when God formally made the covenant with Abraham. Though the promises may appear to be about nothing more than Isaac, Israel, Canaan and David, Jesus taught His disciples—and He teaches us—that *all* of the oaths God swore to Abraham were ultimately about Him (Christ) and the salvation He would provide for us. So the same New Creation that Adam lost by the Fall was being given to Abraham, and is being given to us, by grace alone through faith alone because of the Last Adam alone.

Unfortunately, many miss the grandeur of God's covenant grace because they begin with their thinking with their own ideas about covenants. Many believe that all biblical covenants are made up of promise and obligation.[40] In addition, the idea is widespread that merit is always and everywhere an unbiblical notion.

But merit simply refers to the worth or value of an action. Merit refers to what an action *deserves*. So if there is no merit, then actions don't deserve anything. Not only does obedience not deserve a reward, but disobedience does not deserve punishment. Those are the consequences of rejecting merit. So in a universe without merit, nothing Abraham is, and nothing he does deserves God's wrath and punishment. But when we take merit away with one hand, we re-introduce it with the other hand in the form of covenant conditions. Those who reject the idea of merit probably think that they have saved God's grace from the errors of legalism and antinomianism (literally "against the Law" or "no need for obedience"). However, rejecting merit only redefines salvation either by making a mockery of God's justice (because no human actions are worth anything) or by making salvation conditioned upon our works (because the need to please God is still felt).

Of course, there is a certain kind of condition involved in the Covenant of Grace. Part of the effect of this covenant is to produce completely righteous people who are fully conformed to Christ's image at the Last Day (and for all eternity).[41] But notice that such righteousness (i.e., works) is the *effect* of salvation and not the cause. Some would see Abraham's circumcision as a work that

---

[40] One recent example of this is Norman Shepherd in his book, *The Call of Grace: How the Covenant Illuminates Salvation and Evangelism* (Phillipsburg: P&R Publishing, 2000), 20. He is certainly not the only one. Almost a decade earlier than Shepherd, Daniel P. Fuller drew the same conclusions in his book *Gospel & Law: Contrast or Continuum? The Hermenutics [sic] of Dispensationalism and Covenant Theology* (Pasadena: Fuller Seminary Press, 1991), 134-145.

[41] Believers will certainly begin to demonstrate that righteousness in this lifetime, before the Last Day. But in this world, the righteousness that we produce will always be imperfect and tainted by sin (cf. Is. 64:6; 1 John 1:8, 10).

Abraham had to do to *cause* him to be right with God. But the condition of the Covenant of Grace works like this: "If you are saved by grace through faith, you will have good works (like circumcision)." So good works are necessary for salvation in the Covenant of Grace, but they are necessary as the *effect* or *evidence* of salvation—not at all as the cause.

Yet after we understand that fundamental difference, there are some other important things to be said about the role of circumcision in the Covenant of Grace. Probably the most important thing to be said is that circumcision was the *sign* of the covenant before Christ (Gen. 17:11). In other words, circumcision was a visible signal to the entire world of which people belonged to God. It was God's way of saying, "These people are my covenant people." Circumcision distinguished between the descendants of Eve and the descendants of the serpent. It was the sign of membership in the Covenant of Grace. So it only makes sense that the covenant would be "broken" by someone who refused to be circumcised. Any male who rejected circumcision was saying in effect, "I do not belong to God; I am not one of His covenant people."

However, the apostle Paul says that circumcision was not only a sign, it was also a *seal* of the righteousness of the faith Abraham had while he was still uncircumcised (Rom. 4:11). As a seal, circumcision confirmed or verified that Abraham was righteous. But take special notice of the fact that Abraham's righteousness was not the righteousness of his own obedience by being circumcised. It was not the obedience of being circumcised. **Abraham's righteousness was the righteousness of *faith*.** As we address the popular concept of conditions in the Abrahamic Covenant (or the Covenant of Grace), we will look more closely at what exactly the righteousness of faith is. But we should also pay close attention to what Paul goes out of his way to say: Abraham was righteous *while he was still uncircumcised*. Therefore, contrary to what some would have us believe, circumcision did not contribute to Abraham's righteousness before God.

In passing, we should notice that circumcision—which visibly set God's people apart from unbelievers as a *sign*, and which confirmed that the circumcised person was righteous as a *seal*— circumcision was not restricted to the elect. For one thing, as human beings, we do not have access to God's knowledge of whom He has chosen and whom He has not chosen. But more importantly, Abraham was not commanded to reserve circumcision only for his sons who *proved* that they were elect. God commanded him to circumcise all the males who were under his family authority. In the same way, his sons who also trusted God's promise were to circumcise all the males who were under their family authority, and so on. Abraham circumcised both Isaac (Gen. 21:4; Acts 7:8) and Ishmael (Gen. 17:23), but only Isaac was elect (Gen. 17:20-21; Rom. 9:6-9). Isaac circumcised both Jacob and Esau, but only Jacob was elect (Gen. 25:21-34; Rom. 9:10-13). So the membership of the Covenant of Grace is not pure. There will be both believers and unbelievers who are visibly identified as God's people. In other words, "covenant" does not mean the same thing as "election" or "predestination." There are more members of the Covenant of Grace than there are members of the elect. We might diagram it like this:

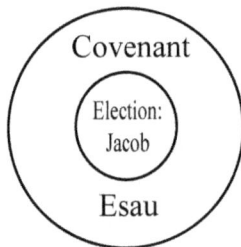

Another problem that many have with the Covenant of Grace is the role of faith, especially as Genesis describes its role in Abraham's justification. When Genesis 15:6 says, "Abraham believed God and it was credited to him as righteousness," some take that to mean that Abraham's *faith* was so amazing that God was impressed and rewarded Abraham with righteousness as a result.

But Abraham—like you and me—was a descendant of Adam's. As a result of Adam's Fall, we are all sinners. The apostle Paul says that by nature, sinners do not believe what God says (Rom. 3:10-18; Eph. 2:1-3). That is because in opposition to the life of the New Creation, we are all born dead in trespasses and sins (Eph. 2:1, 5), enemies of God (Rom. 8:7). If *any* sinful human being is going to believe what God says, it is *only* because God *first* made him alive (Eph. 2:5; Col. 2:13) by giving him the New Birth from above (John 3:3ff.). Even though we deserved His wrath in Hell, God graciously gave us New Birth—New Life—from Heaven so that we would be *able* to believe (i.e., to trust Christ). So nobody would be able to believe God's promises if God did not first give him or her faith (Eph. 2:8-9). Therefore, God not only made promises to Abraham, but He also gave Abraham New Life and faith so that he could trust the promises (Christ). Faith was not a condition that Abraham met so that God's promise would be effective. Faith was a gift that God gave Abraham *because* His promise is effective. So if anyone wants to say that faith is a condition that must be met in order for God's promises to be fulfilled, then we must point out that *God* met the condition by giving Abraham his faith.

Besides, the emphasis in Genesis 15:6 (and Rom. 4:3, 20-22; Gal. 3:6) is not on Abraham's faith, it is on God's promise: "And he [Abraham] believed God and it was credited to him as righteousness." Abraham believed God. He trusted in God. But the faith that Abraham had was not a bare intellectual grasp of God's existence. To illustrate: if I were to say to you, "I believe you"—you would not understand me to be saying that I believe that you exist. When I say, "I believe you," that implies that you have *said* something, and that I believe the content of what you have said.

The same is true when the Bible says that Abraham believed God. God had promised Abraham that Christ would be his descendant (Gal. 3:16) and his King who would lead him into the Promised Land of Heaven. So when Scripture says that Abraham "believed God," it is saying that Abraham believed and trusted in God's *promise*—he trusted in Christ.

But the real question is, When Scripture says, "Abraham believed God and *it* was credited to him as righteousness," what exactly was credited to Abraham? The apostle Paul gives an amazing answer to this question in Romans chapter 4.

Paul begins the chapter by contrasting two different ways of being justified: either by works (v. 2) or by faith (v. 3). By quoting Genesis 15:6, he concludes that Abraham was justified by faith and not by works. But he goes on to explain his reasoning, inspired by the Holy Spirit. There are two kinds of people: those who work to earn their justification, and those who trust Someone else to earn their justification for them. Those who work do not receive their justification based on God's grace, but rather on His justice—because it is given to them as a wage they have merited (v. 4). In contrast, those who are justified based on God's grace do not *work* to merit their justification, but rather they *trust Christ*, and *His* righteousness is credited to them as if it were their own (v. 5). This is the clear answer to our question, What exactly was credited or imputed to Abraham as righteousness? Christ's righteousness—His perfect obedience to God's law—was imputed to Abraham and it is imputed to us by the instrument of faith.

In Romans 3, Paul had just spent the majority of the chapter arguing that every single human being is corrupted by sin—"there is no one who does good; no not even one" (Rom. 3:12). God is just and fair, and our sins deserve punishment. Remember the "checkbook" illustration from the first chapter: we not only have lots of debt (sin), but because of our sin, we cannot produce true and pure good works. That is why, in Romans 4:6, Paul says that *as sinners* we are blessed because God imputes righteousness to us *apart from works.* He then quotes Psalm 32:1-2 to demonstrate that God could have—should have—imputed sin to us. But instead, He has forgiven our sin and covered over it (vv. 7-8).

Paul spends verses 9 through 15 talking about circumcision and keeping the Law. But at verse 16, he returns to Abraham's (and our) justification by grace alone, through faith alone, on account of Christ alone:

> Therefore, it is by faith, according to grace, so that the promise would be guaranteed to all his descendants—not just to those who are of the Law, but also to those who are of the faith of Abraham (who is the father of us all. Just as it is written, "I have made you the father of many nations") in the presence of Him whom He trusted, God, who makes the dead alive and who calls things into being that did not exist. [He] who hoped against hope, believed that he would become the father of many nations according to what was written, "So shall your descendants be." And not weakening in faith, he considered his own body as good as dead since he was about one hundred years old and Sara's womb was barren. But he did not doubt the promises of God in unbelief; rather he was made stronger in his faith, giving glory to God—being fully convinced that He is able to do what He had promised. Therefore, "it was imputed to him for righteousness." Now "it was imputed to him," was not written just for him, but also for us to whom it will be imputed as those who trust Him who raised Jesus our Lord from the dead. (Rom. 4:16-24)

Contrary to those who would add our obedience to faith in Christ as the ground of our justification, the apostle Paul says that the promise was not conditioned upon Abraham's obedience. It was *guaranteed* to Abraham and to us because it was "according to grace" (v. 16). Abraham was not able to boast even about his faith, since it was God who not only provided it, but also strengthened it for him (v. 20). It was not Abraham's *faith* that was imputed to him for righteousness, but it was what God had *promised*: Christ's perfect obedience (vv. 20-24; cf. Rom. 10:10). Sadly, many have it completely backwards. But righteousness is not a *condition* we must meet in order for God to save us; righteousness is a *result* of the salvation of the Covenant of Grace—and faith is merely the instrument that God uses to impute *Christ's* righteousness to us.

In other words, God **promised** Abraham salvation in the life, death and resurrection of Jesus Christ. Abraham believed that promise, and *Christ's perfect obedience* was credited to Abraham as righteousness. Though some would turn faith into a "good work" that we must do in order to be saved, the Bible does not use the word "faith" that way. Especially in the New Testament, faith is almost always *trust in Christ*.[42] Consider the many times that the apostles and disciples called people to "believe on the name of Jesus Christ." So it is not *faith* that is righteous. What Christ *did* by obeying God's Law and submitting to death on the cross—*that* is righteous. **Faith is simply the instrument by which we receive Christ's righteousness.** As an instrument, faith is like open hands that are ready to receive a gift. The open hands are not the most important things—the *gift* is. When you were handed the best gift of your entire life, you didn't say, *Wow! Look at my empty, outstretched hands!* —did you?

---

[42] See B.B. Warfield's article "The Biblical Doctrine of Faith" in *Biblical Doctrines* (Southampton: The Camelot Press Ltd., 1929), 477. He lists the following passages as being the most common NT references to faith: Mt. 18:6; Jn. 2:11; 3:16, 18, 36; 4:39; 6:29, 35, 40; 7:5, 31, 38, 39, 48; 8:30; 9:35, 36; 10:42; 11:25, 26, 45, 48; 12:11, 37, 42, 44, 46; 14:1, 12; 16:9; 17:20; Acts 10:43; 14:23; 19:4; Rom. 10:14; Gal. 2:16; Phil. 1:29; I Pet. 1:8; I Jn. 5:10; cf. Jn. 12:36; 1:12; 2:23; 3:18; I Jn. 5:13.

Even *if* faith were righteousness, it would still be God's gift to Abraham and us. Therefore, it would still be God's righteousness, and not ours. But Ephesians 2:8-9 says, "For it is by grace you have been saved through faith, and this not of your own doing—it is the gift of God—not based on works so that no one may boast." We cannot even boast about our faith because grace, salvation *and faith*[43] are all gifts from God. If He had not given us faith (and the New Birth from Heaven), we would not have believed.

Another mistake that many make is reducing faith to a simple intellectual act of assent.[44] They would appeal to James chapter 2. There, James seems to use the word "faith" in a way that no other New Testament writer uses it. When James uses the word "faith" he seems to mean "a purely mental act," or a bare, intellectual grasp of God's existence. But even demons have *that* kind of faith (James 2:19). So if that is what James means by "faith," then of course faith alone (i.e., a bare, intellectual grasp of God's existence) can't save anyone. If it could, then demons would be saved, too.

---

[43] Many biblical scholars object to including "faith" as one of God's gifts to us. They think that when Paul says, "and *this* not of yourselves..." 'this' refers *only* to salvation. Some even object, noting that the Greek word for "faith" (*pistis*) is feminine in gender, while the word for "this" (*touto*) is neuter in gender. They argue that the two words must agree in gender in order for "this" to refer to "faith." But Dr. Steven M. Baugh of Westminster Theological Seminary in California has pointed out to me, that in Mt. 1:21-23; 8:9-10; 9:27-30; Lk. 22:22-23; Jn. 6:28-29; Eph. 6:1 and 1 Tim. 4:16 all neutralize and put to rest these objections. In the same way that the word "this" refers to the entire action of "being saved by grace through faith," these other passages also have the singular, neuter word "this" referring to an action *as a whole*. Plus, the entire actions referred to by "this" consist of masculine, feminine and neuter genders. Dr. Baugh also notes that this phenomenon is common in extra-biblical Greek as well.

[44] Shepherd, Norman. *The Call of Grace: How the Covenant Illuminates Salvation and Evangelism* (Phillipsburg: P&R Publishing, 2000), 15.

But of all the New Testament authors, the apostle Paul especially uses the word faith to refer to *trust* in the person and work of Jesus Christ for salvation. That is why Paul says that there are only two ways to spend eternity with God in His New Creation Kingdom: faith or works (Rom. 4:4-5; 10:5-10; 11:6; Gal. 3:11-12; 3:18). Over and over again, Paul says that we are justified by faith *apart from* works (Acts 13:39; Rom. 3:20-21, 28; Gal. 2:16)—which is another way of saying that we are justified by trust in Christ (i.e., faith) *alone*.

So when James says, "a man is justified by works and not by faith alone," there are at least two options. The first option is that James plainly contradicts the apostle Paul. But if we believe that the same Holy Spirit inspired both Paul and James, then to say that James contradicts Paul is to say that the Holy Spirit inspired a contradiction and *lied* either through James or through Paul. But God cannot lie, so that option is not open to us. The other option is that James uses the word "justify" differently than Paul. Whereas Paul uses the word "justify" to mean that God has legally *declared* someone to be righteous, most Reformed theologians believe that James uses "justify" to mean someone's *demonstration* of his or her own righteousness. They understand James to mean that *a man demonstrates his faith by his works*. Now all of those Reformed theologians could very possibly be wrong. But on more than one occasion, the Bible uses the word "justify" in the sense of a *demonstration* of right standing with God *by good works*. In Ezekiel 16:51 and 52, Jeremiah 3:11 and Matthew 11:19, people *show* that they are justified (or not justified) by what they do. That option—the *demonstration* of righteousness by works—is certainly much better than the belief that we are actually saved by faith *plus* (non-meritorious) works.

Popular teachers like Norman Shepherd and Daniel P. Fuller believe that the Abrahamic covenant is conditional because "Abraham was commanded to walk before the Lord and to be blameless."[45]   Based on Genesis 18:19 and 26:3-5, these men, and others, believe that Abraham's salvation and our own salvation depends upon our good works.[46]   But as we have pointed out before, Abraham did not work to meet any conditions so that God's promise could be fulfilled. Abraham did good works *because* God's promise was sovereign and gracious. Therefore, it was *impossible* for His promise to fail.

But we should take seriously the verses Shepherd mentioned. On the surface, they certainly seem to say that God gave Abraham rewards on the basis of his good works. Yet this brings to light a common problem that many have with covenant theology. Instead of understanding all of the covenants as being related to Adam and Christ as the two covenant representatives of humanity, covenant seem to be explained as though each individual stands before God on his or her own. Instead of understanding the Bible as the tale of two Adams (the condemnation of all because of the first Adam and the redemption and consummation of many because of the Last Adam), those who misunderstand the relationship of the covenants seem to think that all covenants are up for grabs, so it is "every man for himself." But we must always remember that the entire Bible—from Genesis to Revelation—is about Jesus Christ (Luke 24:25-49; John 5:39-47; 1 Pet. 1:10-12). Even the story of Abraham is about Christ.[47]   Therefore, we may

---

[45] This quote is from Norman Shepherd's book, *The Call of Grace: How the Covenant Illuminates Salvation and Evangelism* (Phillipsburg: P&R Publishing, 2000), 16. Compare Fuller, Daniel P. *Gospel & Law: Contrast or Continuum? The Hermenutics* [sic] *of Dispensationalism and Covenant Theology* (Pasadena: Fuller Seminary Press, 1991), 134-145.

[46] Shepherd, Norman. *The Call of Grace: How the Covenant Illuminates Salvation and Evangelism* (Phillipsburg: P&R Publishing, 2000), 16, 17. Also Fuller, Daniel P. *Gospel & Law: Contrast or Continuum? The Hermenutics* [sic] *of Dispensationalism and Covenant Theology* (Pasadena: Fuller Seminary Press, 1991), 121-145.

[47] Abraham was called to obey God and leave his country and go to a land that God would show him (Gen. 12:1). Christ was called to obey God and leave his

even say that Abraham was a type of Christ. Christ acted on our behalf, and as a type of Christ, Abraham acted on behalf of his family. That is not to say that anybody was ultimately saved because of what Abraham did. But unlike Norman Shepherd, we ought to understand that the story of Abraham's obedience points us to Christ's obedience—because Christ's obedience is the only salvation that is available.

CONCLUSION

In spite of what anyone may say, all covenants are not made up of two parts: God's promise and our obligation.[48] Covenants do not depend upon both God doing His part and us doing our part. God does not need our help to accomplish His purposes. In His word He tells us that He establishes covenants based on justice through works or covenants based on grace through faith—but *never* both (Rom. 11:6; Gal. 3:18). When a covenant is based on justice, God chooses a reward and tells humanity what kind of obedience we must produce in order to receive the reward. God has the right to do that. But in covenants based on grace, God fulfills the required obedience *for* His people, and He produces obedience in them as part of the covenant blessing.

Because of the first man Adam, humanity is fallen and desperately needs salvation. But because of the Last Adam, God promised Abraham and us eternal life in Heaven even though we deserve the worst punishment for our sin. By faith we lay hold of Christ and *all* His benefits—including forgiveness of sins and His righteousness imputed to us (i.e. justification). By God's grace (i.e.,

---

country (Mt. 2:13-15) and go to the ultimate Promised Land (Lk. 24:50-53; Acts 1:2) on our behalf so that we also may live in that Promised Land. [Notice in Mt. 2:13-15 that Jesus is being called to leave the land of *Israel* on the basis of the Hos. 11:1/Num. 24:8 prophecy, "Out of Egypt did I call My Son." God is identifying Israel with the wickedness of Egypt during the Exodus.]

[48] Shepherd, Norman. *The Call of Grace: How the Covenant Illuminates Salvation and Evangelism* (Phillipsburg: P&R Publishing, 2000), 20, 39-40, 44.

demerited favor) we have faith in Christ because God has first given us New Life from above. Because of that New Life and because we love Jesus for what He did in spite of our sin, we can't help but want to obey what God has told us to do.

So to try to make the Abrahamic Covenant of Grace into a covenant of works by introducing conditions to be met and obligations to be fulfilled is to launch an attack on the Gospel of justification by grace alone through faith alone because of Christ alone. Romans 11:6 and Galatians 3:18 make it clear that covenants are either based on justice or on grace, but never both. If we add conditions (or works) to God's Covenant of Grace, then we imply that justification is by faith *and* our works, and we nullify God's promise (Gal. 3:15-18).

So the Abrahamic covenant is relevant for us today because we too, are members of it. How are we members of the Abrahamic covenant? We are members as his descendants who have the same *faith in Jesus Christ* that he did. We are Abraham's "seed" because we belong to Christ by faith (Gal. 3:29). Abraham was justified because he trusted in the Seed (Christ) whom God had promised—and the righteousness of that Seed was imputed to Abraham by faith/trust (Rom. 4:3). We are justified in exactly the same way, except that we have the fulfillment of God's promise. Therefore, we are the "nations" whom God promised to Abraham (Gen. 17:5; Rom. 4:17). We have actually received the promises that God made to Abraham because Christ has fulfilled them—even though Abraham only saw Him from a distance (Heb. 11:8-16).

So to return to our diagram of the covenants and the Kingdom of God, the Abrahamic covenant fits like this:

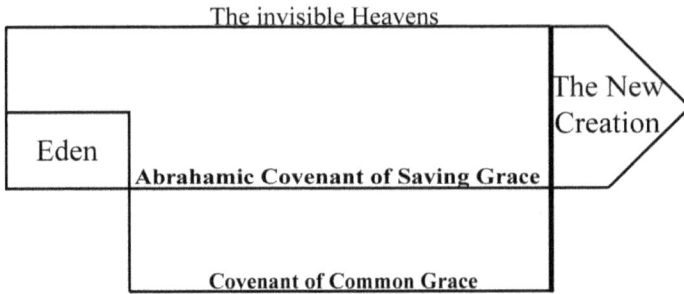

Saving grace—from Genesis 3:15 to Abraham all the way up to the Last Day—has the New Heavens and the New Earth as its goal. The New Creation had been Adam's goal, too. But when he gave up that goal at the Fall, God was still in control. Somehow, the Fall was part of God's plan; and God's answer to the Fall (for His special, covenant people) was the Covenant of Grace. Even if Adam had failed to merit eternal life with God for all of humanity, God would still live with His people forever. God took the initiative to save us in the Covenant of Grace, when what we really deserved was the curse of the Covenant of Works from Creation.

Members of the Covenant of Grace have eternal life in the Kingdom of God to look forward to. The Covenant of Common Grace is God's means of providing stability in the world while He saves His people from their sins. Instead of having a goal like the Covenant of Grace, it will come to an end when Christ returns. But it continues on at the same time as the Covenant of Grace. For example, Abraham lived at peace with uncircumcised people. When he visited foreign nations, he lived as they lived.

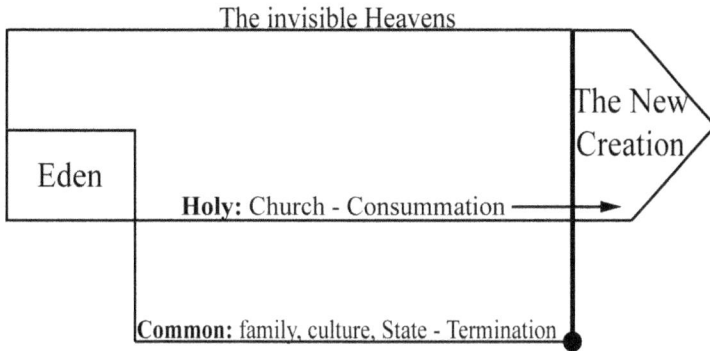

The Church is the only holy institution after the Fall. Its God-given jobs are worship and missions. The covenant people of God are distinct from the world. We are to gather together at least once a week to worship God in the ways He has instructed us. God has also decided to use preaching to call the world out from under Adam's curse and into Christ's Heavenly blessings in the Covenant of Grace (Rom. 10:14; 1 Pet. 1:23-25). But God has given culture, the family and the State (common grace) a very different job. Unlike the worship and missions of the Church, common grace institutions are to simply provide for the survival of creation and humanity. God sends the Church out into the rest of humanity in order to call them to faith in Jesus Christ.

God has set His people (Covenant of Grace) apart from the world (common grace) in a number of ways. In this chapter, we learned that God distinguished His people from the world by circumcision in the Abrahamic covenant. God still distinguishes His people from the world today. In the New Covenant, He does it by baptism. But we, as the holy and distinct people of God still live in this world. We still participate in this creation. So we should enjoy the good gifts that He has given us here. We should not try to "Christianize" what God has made common to believers and unbelievers. Instead, in everything that we do, we should do it all to the glory of God.

The Covenant of Grace

6

The Mosaic Covenant: The Old Covenant of Law

The Mosaic Covenant

When we get to the end of the book of Genesis, the story seems to be left hanging. God had promised Abraham a King (David/Christ), a land (Canaan/Heaven) and a people (Israel/the elect). He confirmed that promise to Abraham's son Isaac in Genesis 21:12 and 26:3-4, and He confirmed it again to Isaac's son Jacob in Genesis 28:13-15 and 35:11-12. In the last chapter of Genesis, Jacob died and was buried in Canaan. But Jacob's son Joseph stayed in Egypt—and even though he recognized the covenant that God had sworn to his great-grandfather Abraham, his grandfather Isaac and his father Jacob (Gen. 50:24), Joseph died in Egypt.

But why does the story seem to end in Egypt and not in the promised land of Canaan? If the end of Genesis does not leave us begging for the answer to this question, certainly the beginning of Exodus does. There, Abraham's, Isaac's, Jacob's and Joseph's children—Israel—become so numerous that the Egyptians and their new Pharaoh were afraid of them and made them all slaves in order to control them. The seed of the first Adam by birth and the seed of the Last Adam by faith—they were not living freely in the land that God had promised them, but they were living as slaves in a foreign land.

Yet God had not forgotten His promise. He had chosen Moses to lead Israel out of slavery and into liberty. He called Moses to confront Pharaoh and threaten him with various curses if he did not release the Israelites. But Pharaoh refused. So God not only punished the Egyptians with many natural disasters, but He also killed their firstborn sons. Yet God did not kill any of the Israelites because they had sacrificed a lamb and smeared its blood over their doorposts as He had instructed.

So Pharaoh finally let Israel leave Egypt. But the way that God told Moses to lead them was blocked by the Red Sea. Of course, that may have appeared discouraging and threatening to the terrified Israelites who wanted to flee from Pharaoh. But this too, was by God's design. God told Moses to lift his staff, and the Red Sea parted so that Israel could walk across to the other side on dry land. Meanwhile, Pharaoh had changed his mind about letting Israel go for the tenth time. So he and some of his military chased after Israel in chariots. But as Israel made it safely to the other side of the Sea and Pharaoh and his army entered the parted waters, God told Moses to stretch out his hand so that the waters returned to normal and drowned the Egyptians. First Corinthians 10:1-2 compares this Red Sea ordeal with the waters of baptism. Yet the Exodus through the Red Sea functioned as a sort of judgment. Israel passed through the parted waters unharmed so as to signify that God had approved or justified them. Pharaoh and his army, however, were drowned, signifying God's condemnation. So when Paul compares the Exodus through the Red Sea with baptism, he indicates that we have passed through the waters of God's judgment safely in Christ—while unbelievers will join Pharaoh in his condemnation on the Last Day.

Through the Red Sea, Moses led Israel out of Egypt and into the wilderness. The Lord led them by a pillar of cloud during the day and a pillar of fire during the night to the base of Mount Sinai. Smoke and clouds hid the mountain as God descended in fire to meet with Moses, and the whole valley shook violently. Just as the journey through the Red Sea was a picture of the end of the world, so Mount Sinai was a picture of the Last Day in miniature. In fact, the Israelites were so terrified, that they begged Moses, "You speak with us and we will listen. But do not let God speak with us lest we die!" (Ex. 20:19).

So God spoke to Moses on Mount Sinai and gave him not only the Ten Commandments, but an entire covenant that He was making with Israel. In one sense, the covenant at Sinai was a continuation of God's covenant with Abraham because He was providing some of Abraham's numerous descendants (Gen. 12:2) with a small picture of their kingdom-inheritance (Gen. 12:1). Yet, in another sense, this covenant was not simply a continuation of the

Covenant of Grace from Genesis 3:15 to Abraham and beyond. Many see the Mosaic covenant as a further unfolding of the Abrahamic covenant.[49] However, we see that the Mosaic covenant not only has different blessings and curses than the Abrahamic covenant, but it operates according to the principles of justice and works as opposed to the Abrahamic covenant's principles of grace and faith. Even though God gave the land of Canaan to Israel out of His kindness in spite of their sin (i.e., grace), Israel had to earn the right to remain in Canaan by their own obedience to the Law (i.e., justice, works). In the history of God's covenants with humanity, the Mosaic covenant is unique because it is typological (i.e., an earthly picture of a heavenly or future reality) – typological of the ultimate, Heavenly, New Creation Kingdom of God. In fact, it is as if Heaven and the Final Judgment could not wait—they broke into history ahead of time.[50] Let's take a look at some of the biblical evidence for this.

THE MOSAIC COVENANT AS A TYPOLOGICAL COVENANT OF WORKS[51]

---

[49] Shepherd, Norman. *The Call of Grace: How the Covenant Illuminates Salvation and Evangelism* (Phillipsburg: P&R Publishing, 2000), 29. Compare also Fuller, Daniel P. *Gospel & Law: Contrast or Contiuum?: The Hermenutics* [sic] *of Dispensationalism and Covenant Theology* (Pasadena: Fuller Seminary Press, 1990), 105.

[50] Of course, this was God's doing. He has decreed when the Last Day will come, but He has also arranged for that Last Day to break in "ahead of schedule" at various times in the history of His covenants.

[51] This has been the classical, Reformed position on the Mosaic Covenant. See Mark W. Karlberg's Ph.D. dissertation *The Mosaic Covenant and the Concept of Works in Reformed Hermeneutics: A Historical-critical Analysis With Particular Attention to Early Covenant Eschatology* (Ann Arbor: 1981; #802493); compare also Robert Rollock's (1555-1599) *Treatise of Our Effectual Calling*; William Pemble's *A Treatise of Justification by Faith* (1625); Edward Fisher's *Marrow of Modern Divinity* (1645); Thomas Boston's (1676-1732) annotations to Edward Fisher's *Marrow*; John Owen's (1616-1683) *An Exposition of the Epistle to the Hebrews*; Amandus Polanus' *Syntagma Theologiae Christianae* (1609); Herman Witsius' (1636-1708) *The Economy*

1. Israel swore the covenant oath. You will recall how in chapter 1 we discussed the significance of who swears the covenant oath. After the Fall, we see that when God swears the oath that covenant is a covenant based on grace. It could not be any other way. The Covenant of Grace that God made formally with Abraham is a perfect example of this. In Genesis 15, God swore to keep the covenantal promises He had made to Abraham. He even threatened Himself with death if He did not keep the covenant. Since it is impossible for God to lie or deal falsely or unfairly with anyone, the covenant was as good as kept and fulfilled. It could not have happened any other way.

But when human beings swear a covenant oath to God, it is a completely different story. Human beings *can* lie and deal falsely and unfairly with God and their neighbors. In fact, after the Fall, human beings *do* lie, cheat and steal because we are bent that way. So when a fallen person swears a covenant oath to God, it can and will be broken. Not only that, but the covenant oath involves taking personal responsibility for the outcome of the covenant ("*If I do the things of the covenant, may I receive its blessings; but if I do not do the things of the covenant, may I receive its curses*"). So whereas in the Covenant of Grace Someone *else* takes personal responsibility for keeping the covenant *for us* (since we are unable to keep it perfectly ourselves), in covenants of works, people solemnly swear to be personally responsible for keeping the covenant *themselves*.

This is exactly what Israel did in the Mosaic covenant. There are numerous examples of this. Exodus 19:8, 24:3 and 7, Deuteronomy 5:27, 26:17, Joshua 24:24 and Nehemiah 10:28-32 all record instances of Israel swearing to keep the covenant that God had made with them. Israel took *personal* (i.e., corporate,

of the Covenants Between God and Man: Comprehending a Complete Body of Divinity; Peter van Mastricht's *Theoretico-practica Theologia* (1725). See www.upper-register.com/papers/works_in_mosaic_cov.pdf for a digest of these authors and their works.

community) responsibility for keeping all of the laws of the Mosaic covenant.

2. The outcome of the covenant depended upon Israel's obedience. There are too many laws in the Mosaic covenant for us to consider them all in detail. But there are two passages that are striking because they hold out the offer of rewards for obedience and threaten curses for disobedience. Leviticus chapter 26 and Deuteronomy chapter 28 look something like this:

If Israel obeys...	If Israel disobeys...
rain and produce	terror, sickness and fever
plenty of food & security	enemies will steal food
peace in your land	enemies will strike you down
no dangerous animals/enemies	animals will kill your children
health, wealth and blessedness	sickness, poverty and cursedness

Israel swore that they would be personally responsible so that if they kept the covenant, they would receive everything in the left column and more—but if they didn't keep the covenant, they would receive everything in the right column and more. Their obedience would *cause* them to receive the blessings and rewards while their disobedience would *cause* them to receive the curses and punishments. Compare the contents of Leviticus 26 and Deuteronomy 28 with the sermons of the apostles in the New Testament sometime. The principles that governed the Mosaic covenant (justice and works) are the complete opposite of the good news of the Gospel of grace.

3. Hosea 6:7. This verse reads, "And they, like Adam, have violated My covenant; there they have acted unfaithfully toward Me." We have already seen that the Covenant of Creation with Adam was a covenant of works. Adam's obedience would have caused him to receive the covenant blessings for us and his disobedience caused him to receive the covenant curses for us. The prophet Hosea is saying that Israel violated the Mosaic covenant *in* *the same way* that Adam violated the Covenant of Creation. So if Adam's disobedience caused him to receive the covenant curses, then Israel's disobedience caused them to receive the covenant curses. So if Adam was involved in a covenant of works, then Israel was also involved in a covenant of works.

4. In order for the Last Adam to merit our salvation, He had to fulfill the same kind of covenant that the first man Adam broke. Adam violated a covenant of works and earned eternal death in Hell for all of his descendants. So the Last Adam was "...born under the Law [Mosaic covenant of works] in order to redeem those who were under the Law so that we could receive the adoption of sons" (Gal. 4:4-5). You and I may not have ever been under the Mosaic covenant, but we are all born under the condemnation of Adam's broken Law-covenant and we who trust Christ alone for our salvation are adopted as God's children.

You see, when Adam broke the Covenant of Creation we were all sentenced to an eternity in Hell. We were under that curse. So we may not have been *personally* obligated to keep the Covenant of Creation, but our covenant representative (Adam) *was*. When he violated the covenant, he violated it for us as well. Therefore, it was as if we had personally violated that covenant. His disobedience—his demerit—was imputed to us as our own. The death that was threatened against Adam for his disobedience in Genesis 2:17 is the death that characterizes our existence in this creation (both in body and in spirit). That is why we were under the curse of the Covenant of Creation. But "Christ has redeemed us from the curse of the Law having become a curse for us. As it is written, 'Cursed is everyone who hangs from a tree.'" (Gal. 3:13).

But the Covenant of Creation was broken and over long before Christ ever came into this world. So how could He redeem us from the curse of the Law if that original covenant of works was no longer in operation? He redeemed us from the curse of the Law of the Covenant of Creation because the Law of the Mosaic covenant was also based on justice and works. Both covenants were covenants of works. The covenant into which Christ was born (Mosaic covenant) had to be based on works like the Covenant of Creation so that He could redeem us from the curse of the Law.

5. The apostle Paul says quite plainly that the Law is not based on faith or grace, but on works and justice. In both Romans 10:5 and Galatians 3:12, Paul makes it clear that the Law is not based upon grace, but upon works. It is important to note that when Paul talks about "Law" or "the Law" he is almost always referring to the Mosaic covenant. With that in mind, let's look at these two verses.

Romans 10:5 tells us, "For Moses writes that the person who does [the works of] the righteousness of the Law shall live by those works." Both Romans 10:5 and Galatians 3:12 quote from Leviticus 18:5. We will look at that Old Testament passage shortly. But for now, it is important to recognize that Paul says that "life" in the Old, Mosaic covenant came by obedience to the Law. How were God's people to "live" under the Mosaic covenant? By doing the works of the righteousness of the Law.

Galatians 3:12 says almost exactly the same thing. However, this time, Paul contrasts the Covenant of Grace with the Mosaic Covenant. He says:

> Now, [the fact] that the Law can in no way justify in the presence of God is clear because "The righteous shall live by faith." But the Law is not based on faith. Instead, "the person who does the works [of the Law] shall live by them." (Gal. 3:11-12)

Here, Paul is contrasting two kinds of "life." In verse 11, he quotes Habakkuk 2:4—"the righteous shall *live* by faith." In verse 12, he quotes Leviticus 18:5—"the person who does the works [of the Law] shall *live* by them." One Old Testament passage has people living by faith and another Old Testament passage has people living by works. What does this mean?

Many popular theologians are staunchly opposed to the idea of living in covenant with God on the basis of works.[52] Therefore, like others[53] who are opposed to the concept of merit, they simply assert that Paul is quoting the Jewish *misunderstanding* of the Law.[54] The problem with that assertion is that the context of these verses

---

[52] "God does not, and never did, relate to his people on the basis of a works/merit principle." See his book *The Call of Grace: How the Covenant Illuminates Salvation and Evangelism* (Phillipsburg: P&R Publishing, 2000), 60. Compare Daniel P. Fuller's comments in his book *Gospel & Law: Contrast or Contiuum?: The Hermenutics [sic] of Dispensationalism and Covenant Theology* (Pasadena: Fuller Seminary Press, 1990), 141. There, he says that if his (Fuller's) conclusions are correct, covenant theologians must stop using the term "covenant of works."

[53] Compare the works of representatives of the New Perspectives on Paul like E.P. Sanders, James D.G. Dunn, N.T. Wright, representatives of the Federal Vision like John Barach, Randy Booth, Tim Gallant, Mark Horne, Jim Jordan, Peter Leithart, Rich Lusk, Jeff Meyers, Ralph Smith, Steve Wilkins, Douglas Wilson, and others like Daniel Fuller and John Piper (cf. his books *Desiring God: Meditations of a Christian Hedonist* and *Future Grace*; we are glad, however, to see his change of perspective in books like *The Future of Justification: A Response to N.T. Wright* and *Counted Righteous in Christ: Should We Abandon the Imputation of Christ's Righteousness?*).

[54] Shepherd, Norman. *The Call of Grace: How the Covenant Illuminates Salvation and Evangelism* (Phillipsburg: P&R Publishing, 2000), 37-38. Strangely, one of Shepherd's reasons for refusing to believe that Paul is calling the Mosaic covenant a covenant of works in Rom. 10:5 and Gal. 3:12 is that "Paul is writing from the perspective of the new covenant." But why should that make any difference given Shepherd's understanding of "the covenant"? For Norman Shepherd, all covenants are made up of two parts: promise and obligation. In *The Call of Grace* he says that about the Abrahamic covenant, the Mosaic Covenant and the New covenant. In spite of the fact that he seems to have a decent grasp of *some* of what makes the New covenant *new* (in his chapter on the New covenant), his definition of covenant—promise and obligation—would seem to make the New covenant simply a more modern version of the Mosaic covenant.

does not give us any hint that Paul is explaining a Jewish misunderstanding of the Law. In fact, just the opposite is true. The context of Romans and Galatians seem to indicate that Paul is giving us his *inspired* interpretation of the Law *as it was revealed to Moses.*

But that still brings us back to the question, What does it mean that Habakkuk 2:4 says that "the righteous shall *live* by faith," while Moses in Leviticus 18:5 says that "the person who does the works [of the Law] shall *live* by those works"? The answer lies in the context of Habakkuk 2 and Leviticus 18. In Habakkuk chapter 2, the prophet speaks of the ultimate Kingdom of God in the New Heavens and the New Earth. He is describing the *future.* God's people will live in the ultimate Kingdom of God only by faith in the Last Adam. But in Leviticus 18, Moses is not talking about the *ultimate* Kingdom of God. He speaks over and over again about "the land"—the land of Canaan. Unlike Habakkuk, Moses is talking about the *typological* kingdom of God within the borders of Canaan. Israel had to earn the right to remain in the typological kingdom of God by obedience to the law of the Mosaic Covenant.

The blessings and curses of Leviticus 26 and Deuteronomy 28 are even more clear about "life" and "living" in the promised land of Canaan. If Israel did the works of the Law, they would enjoy a good, long life in Canaan (Lev. 26:1-13; Dt. 28:1-14). But if Israel did not do the works of the Law, Canaan would wither away and Israel's enemies would defeat them and carry them off into captivity. Note well that the goal of the Mosaic covenant was *not* the Heavenly Kingdom of God. We will search the Old Testament in vain if we are looking for any place where the Israelites are told "if you keep the Law, you will go to Heaven; but if you break the Law you will go to Hell."

So the "life" that Romans 10:5 and Galatians 3:12 are talking about is not *eternal* life. Yet many seem to think that if the Mosaic covenant is a covenant of works, then Israel would have been trying to *earn* their salvation the way workers earn their wages.[55] Of course God did not offer eternal life for good works in the Mosaic covenant. God did not even offer *Canaan* (the typological Heaven) for good works in the Mosaic covenant, because Canaan was a small part of His gracious gift He had promised in the Abrahamic covenant. Yet Leviticus 18:5, Deuteronomy 28 and Leviticus 26 make it clear that God offered Israel the ability to *stay* in Canaan and to *enjoy* the comforts of this life there *on the basis of their works.*

WHAT ABOUT GRACE DURING THE TIME OF THE MOSAIC COVENANT?

What we have seen so far about the Mosaic covenant as a typological covenant of works answers the objections of many popular, contemporary covenant theologians. But they do raise some valid questions about the relationship between the Mosaic covenant and the Abrahamic covenant. If God promised Canaan to Abraham by grace, then wouldn't it nullify His promise if He made Israel work to keep Canaan?

The apostle Paul asks this same question in Galatians chapter 3. His answer is fascinating. He says:

> Brethren, I am speaking in human terms: even though it involves a merely human last will and testament, nevertheless no one can nullify it or introduce anything new to it once it has been solemnly ratified. But the promises were spoken to Abraham and to his Seed—it does not say 'and to

---

[55] Shepherd, Norman. *The Call of Grace: How the Covenant Illuminates Salvation and Evangelism* (Phillipsburg: P&R Publishing, 2000), 26, 36. Compare also Fuller, Daniel P. *Gospel & Law: Contrast or Contiuum?: The Hermenutics* [sic] *of Dispensationalism and Covenant Theology* (Pasadena: Fuller Seminary Press, 1990), 109-110.

seeds' as if he were speaking of many descendants, but he is speaking of one—'and to your Seed' who is Christ. And this is what I am saying: the Law—which came 430 years after the covenant that had already been ratified—did not make it invalid so that it nullified the Promise. For if the inheritance was based upon the Law, then it was no longer based upon the Promise—but God graciously gave it to Abraham by the Promise (Gal. 3:15-18).

Paul is saying that if we can't nullify or introduce anything new into human last wills and testaments once they have been legally put into force, then *how much more* is God's covenant with Abraham unable to be nullified or to have anything else introduced into it once it was ratified by God's solemn oath? God did, indeed, ratify the covenant with Abraham, making it legally binding (Gen. 15). Therefore, the Law (the Mosaic covenant) which came 430 years after He had confirmed the Abrahamic covenant to Jacob (Gen.15:13ff.; Ex. 12:40ff.), could not nullify the Abrahamic covenant. Not only that, but since the Abrahamic covenant was already legally binding, the Mosaic covenant *could not be introduced into the Abrahamic Covenant of Grace* (Gal. 3:15). And this is where Paul drives the point home with ruthless force: if the inheritance (the ultimate, Heavenly Kingdom of God) were based upon keeping the Mosaic covenant of Law, then it could no longer be based upon God's sovereign, gracious promise to Abraham. However, Paul says, the fact is that God gave Abraham the Kingdom inheritance based on His sovereign, gracious promise. Therefore, the ultimate Kingdom of God was not the goal of the Mosaic covenant because it was already the goal of the Abrahamic Covenant of Grace.

Some illustrations might be helpful. Even though we will see that there are important differences between the Abrahamic covenant and the New covenant, we can still confidently say that after the Fall, anyone who would be right with God would be saved by grace alone through faith alone because of Christ alone. In the last chapter, we already established that because of the promise in Genesis 3:15 and the formal covenant that God made with Abraham and the elect in Christ, the Covenant of Grace runs from the Fall until the Last Day (when all of the elect will have been gathered in). So we might represent the Covenant of Grace like this:

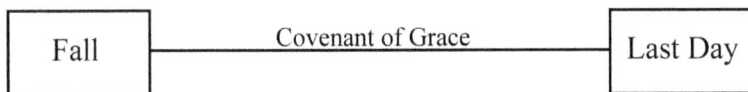

```
┌──────────┐                                    ┌──────────┐
│          │              Covenant of Grace     │          │
│   Fall   ├────────────────────────────────────┤ Last Day │
│          │                                    │          │
└──────────┘                                    └──────────┘
```

But many modern covenant theologians want to insist that the Mosaic covenant is identified with that line above. They believe that the Mosaic Covenant was completely and *only* part of the Covenant of Grace. Yet Paul says that the Mosaic covenant was based upon works and justice (Rom. 2:13; Rom. 10:5; Gal. 3:12). Therefore, it is *impossible* for the Mosaic covenant to be included in the Covenant of Grace because grace is the opposite of justice.[56]

Galatians 3:19 says that the Law was *added* to provoke covenant violations. It is obvious from Paul's argument in verses 15 through 18 that the Law cannot be included in the Covenant of Grace. So how was it "added"? In Romans 5:20 Paul says: "But the

---

[56] The Westminster Confession of Faith recognizes that there is a radical difference between the principle that governs the Covenant of Grace and the principle that governs the Mosaic covenant (works). This comes out clearly in the Scripture proofs that the Confession offers in support of the original covenant of works at creation with Adam. Chapter 7, section 2 of the Confession cites Galatians 3:12 as an instance of a covenant of works—and Galatians 3:12 is clearly referring to the Mosaic covenant because it quotes from Leviticus 18:5. This section also cites Romans 5:14, 20 and Rom. 10:5 as evidence that "life" was held out to Adam (Covenant of Creation based on works)—yet these verses refer to the Mosaic covenant just as clearly as Galatians 3:12. Finally, the Confession cites Galatians 3:10 as proof that "life" is attained in a works covenant "upon condition of perfect and personal obedience"—yet this verse quotes Deuteronomy 27:26, thus linking it to the Mosaic covenant also.

Law *came in alongside* so that covenant violations might increase..."
(emphasis mine) The Law was not part of the Covenant of Grace.
We might say that the Mosaic covenant was the great parenthesis in
covenant history. It was "added" alongside, next to or parallel to the
Abrahamic covenant[57] like this:

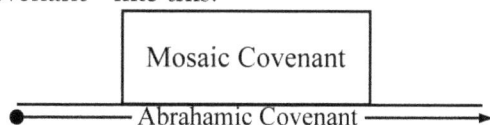

```
          ┌─────────────────────────┐
          │     Mosaic Covenant     │
  ●───────┴── Abrahamic Covenant ───┴──────────►
```

So the Covenant of Grace continued on right next to the
Mosaic Covenant. The Covenant of Grace had the Heavenly
Kingdom of God as its goal. But the Mosaic covenant turned out to
be a typological version of that Heavenly Kingdom. The elect
members of the Covenant of Grace are destined to receive the
Kingdom based on God's grace in Christ. Yet even though Israel
received Canaan based on God's grace to Abraham, they had to
keep the Mosaic Law in order to stay in Canaan and enjoy the land
flowing with milk and honey.

But as Israel entered the land of Canaan we see another
interesting feature of the Mosaic covenant. Unlike Abraham who
lived at peace with uncircumcised unbelievers (Gen. 12:5-20; Gen.
20), Israel was commanded to put every last Canaanite to death with
the sword (see the book of Joshua). They were not to slaughter
every nation on earth, but the borders of Canaan defined the
territory that they were to take by violence. In a certain sense,
Heaven did not wait, and neither did the Final Judgment. In types

---

[57] Virtually all of the Greek lexicons support this. Of the Greek word *pareiselthen*
(come in alongside) Bauer, Danker, Arndt and Gingrich says, "*come in* as a side
issue, of the law, which has no primary place in the Divine Plan." The
Theological Dictionary of the New Testament says "This is a significant word in
Rom. 5:20, where the law has 'come in' as it were parenthetically (to increase
sin)." Liddell and Scott's says *pareiselthen* means "to come or go in beside."
Moulton and Milligan says that it means to "come in from the side" or "come in
to the side of a state of things already existing."

and shadows—with earthly pictures—the great and terrible Last Day came ahead of time for the Canaanites. Just as Jesus will sentence all unbelievers to Hell at the Final Judgment, so Joshua and Israel sentenced the unclean Gentiles to death by the edge of the sword.

But what does this mean for the covenant of common grace that we learned about in chapter 3? It means that within the borders of Canaan, common grace was suspended. Outside Canaan, people continued to live and work and have children as they had since the Fall. We see this illustrated in greater detail when the Scriptures describe Israel living in captivity in a foreign land. In that situation, they were not to bring about typological judgment. They were to live at peace with their captors.

But the death of non-Israelites is not the only thing that indicates that common grace was temporarily suspended in Canaan. God commanded that even circumcised Israelites were to be put to death for many different kinds of violations of the Mosaic covenant. That was because the Mosaic covenant was a theocracy. Theocracy means more than simply "the rule or reign of God." Theocracy means that *everything*—from culture to the worshiping community—*all* institutions are combined into one holy system. It also refers to the *realm* in which God rules and reigns.

So Israel dwelt in the Mosaic theocracy in Canaan for a while. But Canaan was not Heaven. Canaan is part of this fallen creation, and the Israelites were fallen creatures like their father Adam. And Israel did what sinners do: they broke God's Law. In fact, they didn't even obey God as they entered and conquered Canaan. God had told Israel to destroy absolutely everything. But an Israelite named Achan could not resist keeping some gold and silver for himself. So Israel lost in battle against some of the Canaanites as God's just and fair punishment for their sin.

But Achan's sin was not Israel's only violation of the Mosaic covenant. Soon disobedience was a way of life for Israel. Since covenants legally bind God and man, God sent covenant lawyers called prophets to prosecute His covenant lawsuit against Israel. The prophets confronted Israel with God's covenant Law (Genesis - Deuteronomy) and its offer of a long and happy life in Canaan for their obedience as well as its threat of desolation and captivity for their disobedience. Passages like Leviticus 26 and Deuteronomy 28 provided the prophets with a clear summary of God's demands in the Mosaic Covenant.

After listing God's covenantal expectations of Israel, the prophets turned to Israel's history—recorded in Joshua through Esther—as evidence of the specific ways in which Israel had violated the Mosaic covenant. They charged Israel with disobedience and infidelity to God and His Law, and they warned Israel that the curses of the covenant would arrive soon if they did not mend their ways.

Yet this message of impending doom was not the only thing the prophets brought to Israel. The prophets were unique men because they had the privilege of being taken up, by God, into His Heavenly council (Is. 6; Ezek. 1-2). From the vantage point of God's Heavenly courtroom, they received not only the message they were to bring, but a vision of the New Covenant and the Consummation. One of the interesting features of the prophets' messages about life in the New Covenant and in the Consummation is that they tend to describe them in terms of the typological kingdom in Canaan (Is. 65:17-25; Micah 4). When they talked about Heaven, they described it like the land of Canaan. When they talked about Final Judgment, they described it in terms of swords and other ancient weapons. When they talked about the perfection of the ultimate Kingdom of Heaven, they described it like a land in which people lived for a long time and enjoyed its "milk and honey."

Sadly, however, Israel was not interested in repentance. So God followed through with His threat of punishment by desolation and exile (2 Chron. 10-36; 2 Kings 17ff.). Israel's enemies came in and plundered the land, brutalized the people and then carried them off as captives. They were forced to live outside the promised land as the slaves of uncircumcised people. Eventually they were able to return, but Israel had failed miserably at keeping the Mosaic typological covenant of works.

BUT WHAT IS SO WRONG WITH SEEING THE ENTIRE MOSAIC COVENANT AS PART OF THE COVENANT OF GRACE?

Most popular, contemporary covenant theologians want to deny that the Mosaic Covenant was based upon the principle of simple justice so that its blessings and curses were conditioned upon Israel's works. They seem to think that this would mean that people were earning something from God—and in their minds, that would be wrong. What we have said about the Mosaic covenant—namely that it was about the land of Canaan and *not* about Heaven—already answers most of their objections. But we will answer a few of their specific concerns.

First, many see the Mosaic covenant as having been established in fulfillment of the covenant made with Abraham.[58] It is true that God *gave* Canaan to Israel because it was a small part of His promise to Abraham. But the Mosaic covenant was not about *receiving* Canaan based upon good works. It was about *staying* in Canaan and *enjoying* its many blessings based upon good works. So this concern completely misses the point of the Mosaic covenant.

Another point that many are jealous to guard is that the Mosaic covenant is a covenant of promise.[59] It is true that the

---

[58] For example, see Shepherd, Norman. *The Call of Grace: How the Covenant Illuminates Salvation and Evangelism* (Phillipsburg: P&R Publishing, 2000), 27.

[59] Ibid., 30. Note also, that Shepherd says that God "actually wants to forgive those who sin against him, even though they do not deserve to be forgiven" (p. 34). One of Shepherd's central tenets is the denial of merit as a theological

sacrificial system is more compatible with the underlying Covenant of Grace. After all, since the Fall—from Abel to Abraham—the covenant community had been offering sacrifices for sin. In this we see that the Mosaic covenant is a complex thing. However, the prominent feature of the Mosaic covenant is, as Paul says: "Do this and live" (Gal. 3:12; Rom. 10:5). In fact, according to the Apostle Paul's inspired interpretation of the Mosaic covenant in Galatians 3:18: if the inheritance is based upon the Mosaic Law, then it is *no longer* based upon the Abrahamic Promise. Yet God gave the inheritance to Abraham based on His Promise. So contrary to this concern, the apostle Paul gives us one of two choices: the inheritance either comes by the Mosaic covenant of Law and works or by the Abrahamic covenant of grace and Promise—not both. But in fact, it is no choice at all because he tells us that God gave Abraham (and us) the inheritance based on His Promise.

Now that we have answered these concerns, there are two main reasons why it is a threat to the Gospel of justification by faith alone if we say that the Mosaic covenant was a covenant of grace. First, if the Mosaic covenant were part of the Covenant of Grace, then what it said to Israel, it would also say to us (because we are also members of the Covenant of Grace). So when Moses offered rewards for good works (Lev. 26:1-13; Dt. 28:1-14) and threatened curses for disobedience (Lev. 26:14-46; Dt. 28:15-68), we would be tempted to understand Moses as offering and threatening the same things to us. We would naturally think that we would be right with

---

category. Elsewhere, he has said, "There is no question of our desert [i.e. "deserving"], Norman Shepherd, "Man Alive! Creation and Covenant," *Life in Covenant with God* audio tape lecture series presented at the French Creek Family Bible Conference, Sandy Cove, Northeast Maryland, summer 1981, Tape 1, (Philadelphia: Westminster Theological Seminary, 1981). It is ironic that a man who claims not to believe in merit *does* believe that Israel didn't *deserve* to be forgiven. In other words, Shepherd seems to believe that Israel does deserve something: punishment. Sadly, he only implicitly allows for negative demerit/justice (condemnation) and not positive merit/justice (justification).

God—or that God would be pleased with us—if we obeyed all of His commandments perfectly. We would also conclude that God is always ready to punish us as soon as we sin.

But that is not the good news of the Gospel. The Gospel tells us that God is pleased with *Christ's* works on our behalf (Phil. 3:9)—not our own sin-stained deeds. The Gospel also tells us that God punished Christ for the sins that we deserve to be punished for (Gal. 3:13; 2 Cor. 5:21; Rom. 3:24-26). Even though God's grace causes us to do good works, God does not deal with us on the basis of our own works. That is part of what makes the news of the Gospel so good! So viewing the Mosaic covenant as a covenant of grace would actually make us begin to believe that we were under a covenant of works—and *that* is bad news for us sinners.

But there is another reason why it would threaten the doctrine of justification by faith alone if we understood the Mosaic covenant as a covenant of grace. This reason focuses on Christ, rather than on us. Remember that Paul says that God gave the inheritance to Abraham based on His Promise and not based on the Law (Gal. 3:18). This is the same as Paul saying that "if it is by grace, then it is no longer by works; otherwise, grace would no longer be grace" (Rom. 11:6). So when the second person of the trinity became incarnate, He would have been born into a covenant based solely on grace. In other words, Jesus would have lived under a covenant of grace.

We have already seen how this is the same as saying that Jesus was a sinner. If grace is *demerited* favor, and if God dealt with Jesus in a covenant based on demerited favor, then that must mean that Jesus had demerits (i.e., sin or covenant violations). Not only is that an error on these popular covenant theologians' part, but according at least to the Athanasian and Chalcedonian creeds it qualifies as heresy. The only other conclusion that we can come to— if the Mosaic covenant was a covenant of grace—is that Jesus *did* keep the Law perfectly, but God did not give him the reward because grace is the opposite of justice. In any case, either option destroys the foundations of the doctrine of justification by faith alone.

CONCLUSION

The Mosaic covenant was a typological covenant of works. When we say that it was typological, we mean that Israel was not working for eternal salvation. Instead, they were working to stay in the promised land of Canaan (because Canaan was a type of Heaven). When we say that it was a covenant of works, we mean that their obedience to the Law caused the covenant blessings while their disobedience to the Law caused the covenant curses—because that is how God arranged the Mosaic covenant.

But this does not make God's promises to Abraham null and void. Of course, if the Mosaic covenant were part of the *same* covenant as the Abrahamic covenant of grace, the Law *would* nullify God's promises. It would be like having somebody put you in her last will and testament to receive one million dollars at absolutely no cost to you. But instead of receiving the money after her death, the lawyers tell you that you must fulfill all kinds of duties and meet all kinds of demands before you can have the money. Fortunately, the Mosaic covenant is *not* part of the same covenant as the Abrahamic covenant of grace. It came in alongside the Abrahamic covenant 430 years later. In other words, the Covenant of Grace runs continuously from Genesis 3:15 until the Last Day. But the Mosaic covenant of works was in effect from Sinai until Christ (Gal. 3:19) at the same time as the Abrahamic covenant of grace.

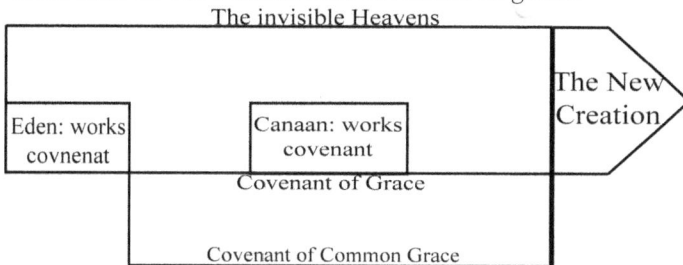

The invisible Heavens

Eden: works covnenat

Canaan: works covenant

The New Creation

Covenant of Grace

Covenant of Common Grace

But when we say that the Mosaic covenant was a *typological* covenant of works, we also mean that a "miniature" version of the Kingdom of God appeared within the borders of Canaan. It was as if God injected or intruded the Heavenly Kingdom into history ahead of time. He has decreed that the Kingdom will not come in power and glory until the end of history. And yet He gave Israel a foretaste of that Kingdom in the Middle East a few thousand years ago.

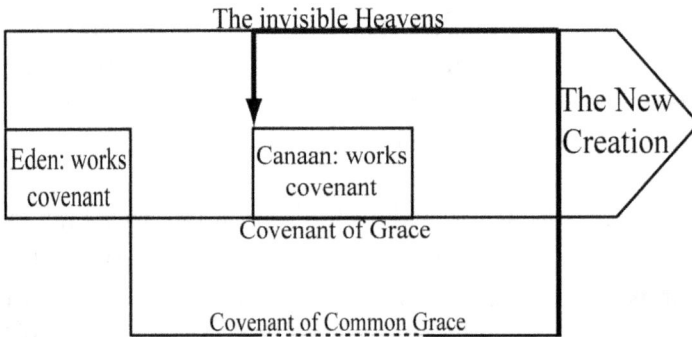

The invisible Heavens

Eden: works covenant

Canaan: works covenant

The New Creation

Covenant of Grace

Covenant of Common Grace

But the Kingdom does not come without judgment—judgment that proves God's people to be righteous, as well as a judgment that condemns unbelievers. The same was true of the Mosaic covenant. When God brought the Kingdom into Canaan and combined everything—family, State, culture, worshiping community—into one holy organization (theocracy), judgment came. So common grace was suspended within the borders of Canaan (dotted line). Of course, the covenant of common grace continued on because the Egyptians, the Assyrians, the Babylonians and every other nation continued to live as people had lived since the Fall. But the Canaanites and all their possessions were supposed to be completely destroyed. Even disobedient Israelites were to be put to death for violating God's Law (cf. Lev. 18-20). Everything in a theocracy is holy.

So even though Israel was under a covenant of works in the Mosaic covenant, they were not working for justification in the ultimate sense. They were sinners like the rest of us. Any attempt at trying to merit their justification as sinners would have been doomed to failure. Instead, Israel was supposed to be working to stay in Canaan. Their "justification" (Rom. 2:13) would have been the right to remain in the promised land. However they confused the typological kingdom for the ultimate Kingdom of Heaven. They began to think that if they if kept the Law, they would be eternally right with God.

But the apostle Paul warns us not to make the same mistake. In Romans chapter 10, he tells us not to imagine that we can please God by our own works. Israel may have looked at their typological covenant of works and they may have assumed that they could spend eternity in the Heavenly Kingdom by keeping the Law. But Christ has become one of us (Rom. 10:6) in order to merit the ultimate Kingdom for us. The proof that He merited it is in His resurrection (Rom. 10:7). So Christ's life, death and resurrection are the only things that can justify us before God.

The Mosaic Covenant

7

The New Covenant: The Triumph of the Last Adam

The New Covenant

The Old Testament left us with multiple prophets prophesying to captive Israelites in foreign countries. Many years passed, and some of the Jews returned to the land of Canaan. But about 400 years after the book of Malachi was written, the very last prophet of the Old Covenant came to announce the arrival of the Lord and His Kingdom. John the Baptizer came to call Israel to repentance before the Judgment. Like the other prophets, John too, was put to death and few Jews believed him.

Israel had been expecting the Messiah because the prophets had talked about Him. But they had not expected the Messiah to be like Jesus. They were looking for a king who would become an important political figure, dominating the world by the edge of his sword. They were looking for a mighty warrior like David who would rush fearlessly into battle with the legions of the Roman Empire—and who would be the only one left standing.

That is why the Jews completely overlooked Jesus as the One who had revealed Himself not only in the words, but also in the people and events of the Old Testament. Far from importance (as the world counts importance), the Messiah was born to poor parents, and His first few nights were spent sleeping in a feeding trough for livestock. Instead of being hailed as King, he had to be whisked away to Egypt for safety. A life story that began like this might tempt us to look elsewhere for the One who would accomplish God's purposes. But if we give in to that temptation, we will join unbelieving Jews in missing the One who radically changed history *and* eschatology.

You see, Jesus is the second person of the Trinity who humbled himself by taking on a human nature—by becoming a man. This was necessary because sin was introduced into God's good creation by the first man, Adam. Humanity's first covenant representative fell, and earned death, judgment and condemnation for us all. Not only was Adam's sin (demerit) imputed to us, but he also left us utterly without the meritorious good works that we needed to withstand God's righteous judgment. Therefore, because the first man Adam caused this situation, salvation required *another* man, the second man (1 Cor. 15:47)—the Last Adam (1 Cor. 15:45)—to succeed at keeping God's covenant on behalf of God's people.

As a result, the story of Jesus' life in covenant with God strikingly resembles the story of Adam's life in covenant with God. Adam had been put on probation in the Covenant of Creation. The fruit of the tree of the knowledge of good and evil was the test of that probation. If he abstained from the fruit as God commanded, he would pass his probation. But if he ate that fruit, he would fail. In the same way, Jesus was put on probation almost immediately upon beginning His ministry. The Spirit drove Him out into the wilderness to fast for forty days and forty nights (Mk. 1:12). So the probation of the Last Adam involved abstaining from *all* food. But it was not limited to food.

Just as the devil tempted Adam and his wife to violate God's covenant, the devil also tempted the Last Adam. Satan used the ideas of food, doubting God's faithfulness and borrowed power to try to lure Jesus into the same kind of covenant violation as Adam. But as the Last Adam, Jesus resisted those temptations and passed His probation. Ironically the Father gave His approval *before* His Son had even begun His probation. Jesus' success was so certain, that at His baptism the Father announced, "This is My beloved Son with whom I am well-pleased" (Mt. 3:17).

Now, because of His success, the Last Adam would be involved in something that the first Adam had only dreamed about: the arrival of the Kingdom. In fact, the first thing the New Testament records Jesus saying after His temptation is: "The time is fulfilled and the Kingdom of God is at hand. Repent and believe in the Gospel" (Mk. 1:15). Immediately, Jesus went about the work of choosing twelve disciples who would not only learn from Him, but whom He would send out to preach the Gospel to the world.

Because the members of the Kingdom would come from believing the Gospel they preached, the disciples would become the heads of the New twelve tribes (Mt. 19:28; Lk. 22:30; Rev. 21:14) of the New Israel (Gal. 6:16) of the New Covenant.

Toward the end of His time with His disciples, Jesus made an important announcement about the New Covenant when He instituted the Lord's Supper. When he instituted the wine as one of the two elements in the Holy Supper, He said that the cup was the New Covenant in His blood (Lk. 22:20). Obviously, He was talking about His death on the cross. His sacrificial death in our place for our sin would mark the ratification of the New Covenant (Heb. 9:11-17).

But the ratification of the New Covenant caused a radical change in history and eschatology. It changed history because the time of waiting on God's promises was over. The Last Adam had come not only to correct the problem of the Fall by His sacrifice of Himself on the cross, but He had also come to earn the right to enter into the ultimate Kingdom of God. The time of having a fallen priest butcher animals to sacrifice for sins every year was over because the High Priest offered Himself as the single sacrifice who actually *removed* sin permanently (Heb. 10). The time of going to the temple to meet with God through a fallen priest was over because in Christ the High Priest, God has come to tabernacle with us (John 1:14). The time of the shadows was over because the sun had begun to dawn (Col. 2:17). The time of promises was over because the reality of those promises had arrived in Jesus. The New Covenant marked the time of fulfillment (Mk. 1:15; Gal. 4:4).

The ratification of the New Covenant also changed eschatology. The saints of the Old Testament saw the end of time as one event.[60] They anticipated the arrival of the Messiah who would bring final judgment on the world (Is. 13:6-16; 26:20-21;

---

[60] The following two modified diagrams are borrowed from p. 38 of Geerhardus Vos' book *The Pauline Eschatology* (Grand Rapids: Eerdmans, 1953).

Ezek. 38:18-23; Mal. 4:1) and who would resurrect the righteous from the grave (Dan 12:2; Ex. 3:6/Mat. 22:29-32).

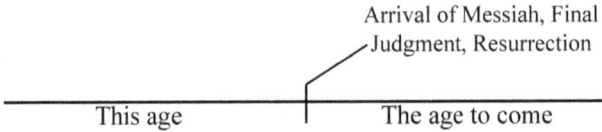

```
                                 Arrival of Messiah, Final
                               ⸺Judgment, Resurrection
 _____⌐_____
        This age            |       The age to come
```

The prophets often referred to this single event as "the latter days," (Dan. 11:40; Is. 2:2; Ezek. 38:16) or "the Day of the Lord" (Amos 5:18; Is. 2:12). So Old Testament believers expected the final judgment and the resurrection to come at the very end of world history—at the latter days, the Day of the Lord.

But when the Last Adam ratified the New Covenant, the end of the world broke into history. Jesus did not deserve to die. He had obeyed God. He had kept the Law perfectly at all times. According to the principle of justice,[61] Jesus deserved to live. But as the Last Adam, He was our representative. He would have to take upon Himself whatever punishment we deserved. According to the curse of Genesis 2:17, Adam earned final judgment—eternal death in Hell—for us. The covenant of common grace had postponed that final judgment. But when Jesus died on the cross, the final judgment of the Last Day—the judgment that *we* deserved—came crashing in upon *Him*. The ultimate justice of God that we were expecting to receive at the very end of history broke into history around 33 A.D. for God's people.

---

[61] Remember the Covenant of Redemption (Ch. 3) and the Mosaic Typological Covenant of Works (Ch. 6). Just as the first Adam related to God in terms of a covenant of works, so the Last Adam related to the Father in terms of a covenant of works. From all eternity, the Father had offered the Son life in the Kingdom with His elect people on the condition of His perfect obedience. So, when the Son entered history as a man, He found Himself under a covenant in which the earthly *picture* of the Kingdom had to be *retained* by perfect obedience.

But that was not all. Jesus still deserved to live for His personal and perfect obedience to His Father—and His Father is not unjust. So three days after Jesus died on the cross, the Father raised Him from the dead by the power of the Holy Spirit. At the beginning of Jesus' ministry, His Father had *declared* that Jesus was justified (Mt. 3:17). Now at the end of Jesus' ministry, His Father *demonstrated* that Jesus was justified by rewarding Him with New Life (1 Tim. 3:16). Jesus did not simply come back to life. As the reward for His perfect obedience, the Father bestowed upon Jesus the kind of life that is necessary for existence in the ultimate, Heavenly Kingdom of God. The resurrection body of Jesus matches the description of New Creation bodies in Revelation 21 and 22.

So everything that God's people had been expecting at the end of history came ahead of time for the Last Adam.

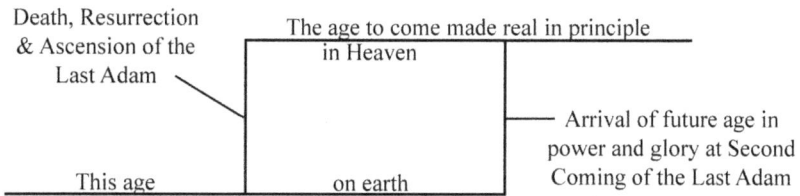

```
Death, Resurrection          The age to come made real in principle
& Ascension of the                    in Heaven
Last Adam
                                                    ─── Arrival of future age in
                                                        power and glory at Second
      This age              on earth                    Coming of the Last Adam
```

God's just judgment of the Last Day fell upon Christ on the cross. The Last Adam had His own righteousness and so He did not remain in the grave—the resurrection of the Day of the Lord was given to Him ahead of time. But that was not all. The Last Adam actually entered into the ultimate Kingdom of God when He ascended into Heaven (Ps. 110; Mk. 16:19). The significance of this must not be missed. The Last Adam—*a human being like us*—entered into the ultimate Kingdom of God *as our representative*. What the first Adam should have done, the Last Adam actually did. So the ultimate Kingdom of God has been inhabited by the Last Adam for the last two-thousand years.

This is what makes the New Covenant *new*. It is not new simply in the sense of the next thing in a series of things—like today is "new" compared to yesterday. The New Covenant is new in the way that the other things in the New Testament are new: New Heavens, New Earth (2 Pet. 3:13), New Jerusalem (Rev. 3:12), New Creation (Rev. 21-22), New Birth/Life (Jn. 3:3, 7).[62] It is a new *kind* of covenant.

We can see some of the new features of the New Covenant in the prophecy of the Old Testament prophet Jeremiah in Jeremiah 31:31-34:

> "Behold, the days are coming," declares the LORD, "when I will make a new covenant with the house of Israel and the house of Judah. It will not be like the covenant which I made with their fathers in the day that I took them by the hand to bring them out from the land of Egypt—My covenant which they broke, though I was a husband to them," declares the LORD. "For this is the covenant which I will make with the house of Israel after those days," declares the LORD. "I will give My Law in their midst and upon their hearts I will inscribe it, and I will be God to them, and they will be My people. And they shall not any longer teach each one his neighbor and each one his brother saying, 'Know the LORD,' because all of them will know the LORD from the least of them

---

[62] The word that is usually translated "again" in "born again" could quite literally be translated "from above." Thus, Jesus was saying that as opposed to being born of the flesh from below, salvation only comes by being born of the Spirit from *above*. This fits perfectly with John's contrast between this world/the world to come, kingdoms of this world/Kingdom of Heaven, life of this creation/life of the New Creation, manna in the desert/Bread of Life, chemical water/Living Water, etc.

to the greatest of them—for I will forgive their
iniquities, and their sins I will remember no more."[63]

The feature of the New Covenant that is probably the most familiar
to us in this prophecy is the accomplishment of the forgiveness of
our sins *in history* (Heb. 9:12). Though believers from Genesis 3:15
on have been forgiven of their sins because of their faith in the
promised Seed of the woman, we no longer anticipate the promise.
In Christ the Last Adam, we have the fulfillment of everything for
which our Old Testament brothers and sisters looked. The New
Covenant marks the arrival of the long awaited and long believed
upon sacrifice for our sins.

But part of the newness of the New Covenant in this
prophecy also involves the lack of teaching among the members of
the covenant community. Jeremiah says that this is because the
entire community will know the Lord. But does that then mean
that ministers are acting unbiblically when they teach? Absolutely
not. No one less than the Lord Christ commanded them to teach
(Mt. 28:18-20; see also Eph. 4:11-16; 1 Tim. 3:2; 4:6-16). This
difference between Jeremiah's prophecy and the present phase of
the New Covenant teaches us that we should not limit our
understanding to the limited vision of the Old Testament prophets.
The prophets saw the coming of the Kingdom of God as one, single
event. Based on what God revealed to them, they were unable to
distinguish between a first coming of the Messiah and a second
coming of the Messiah. The vision of the Old Testament prophets
was like our vision on a long stretch of highway. On a road trip,
two distinct mountains will look like one, single mountain with only
one peak from a far distance. But as we approach the "mountain,"
we notice that there are actually *two* mountains with *two* peaks with
a valley in between them. The same kind of phenomenon is true of

---

[63] This translation of the Hebrew text, though partly mine, is mostly that of Dr.
Meredith G. Kline from his seminary course on the prophets from Westminster
Theological Seminary in California.

revelation. From the viewpoint of the prophets, the first and second comings of the Messiah looked like one package (theologians call this "prophetic foreshortening"). But as revelation progressed, we were shown that there are, in fact, two comings of Christ. Not only that, but the *perfection* of the Kingdom will not characterize the New Covenant until Christ comes the second and last time. While the Last Day came ahead of time for Christ, it has not come in perfection, power and glory yet for His people.

And yet, there are some things about the New Covenant that are *not* new. Notice how Jeremiah says that the New Covenant will *not* be like the covenant that He made with Israel ("the covenant which I made with their fathers in the day that I took them by the hand to bring them out from the land of Egypt"). The New Covenant will not be like the Old Covenant because Israel *broke* that covenant (31:32). It was possible for Israel to break the Mosaic covenant because they swore the oath to keep the covenant. After all, we can only break an oath if we first swear an oath. But the New Covenant will not be like that. The Old Covenant was breakable because sinful Israelites swore the oath of that covenant of works. But God Himself swears the oath of the New Covenant. The New Covenant is not unbreakable because of the people who are in the covenant. We know this because God threatens to ultimately break off those people who turn out to be unbelievers (Rom. 11:16-24 cf. also Heb. 10:26-31). Instead, the New Covenant is unbreakable because God swore the oath, and God cannot lie (Heb. 6:13-18). Notice in Jeremiah 31:31-34, that it is God who does the oath-swearing, and God who swears to do the work of the covenant. The New Covenant is not like the Old typological Covenant of works. The New Covenant—like Genesis 3:15 and the Abrahamic Covenant—is a covenant of grace.

Sadly, some see the newness of the New Covenant as simply a more contemporary form of an older covenant. These people see the Mosaic Covenant and the New Covenant as essentially identical, not as opposed to each other in principle.[64] Of course, as we saw in the last chapter—and this cannot be overemphasized—the Mosaic covenant was not about meriting eternal life in the ultimate Kingdom of God. Neither Jeremiah, nor Paul, nor I am saying that anybody has ever been saved from God's wrath by works. The Mosaic covenant was about *keeping* or *retaining* the *typological* kingdom in the land of Canaan. As a result, both the Old and the New Covenants can be based upon opposing principles (justice and grace) without offering *salvation* apart from grace alone through faith alone because of Christ alone.

Those who see all the biblical covenants as essentially one covenant miss the riches of the Last Adam and the covenants leading up to His Kingdom. They flatten the beautiful contours of our salvation into one generic covenant in which we have to be covenant keepers *just like Jesus* (with his help, of course). This strips the Gospel of the glorious principle of federal, covenant representation. According to monocovenantalists (those who believe in one, generic covenant), no longer does the Last Adam merit our salvation because the first Adam forfeited the Kingdom. Instead, on this view, Adam, you, me and Jesus are all equals in the race to keep covenant with God. On this view, Christ does not keep the covenant *for us* (Protestantism), He *helps* us keep the covenant ourselves (Romanism).

Monocovenantalism includes aspects of each covenant in all the rest so that, for example, the obligations of the Mosaic Covenant appear again in much the same way in the New

---

[64] "The new covenant and the Mosaic covenant are not opposed to each other as two different ways of salvation, one offering salvation by faith and the other by works." Shepherd, Norman. *The Call of Grace: How the Covenant Illuminates Salvation and Evangelism* (Phillipsburg: P&R Publishing, 2000), 57. While he is right about Israel not earning salvation by works, he is wrong to refuse to see the principles of justice and works as the main feature of the Mosaic Covenant with the Apostle Paul.

Covenant. Such well-intentioned people want to include our obedience—our good works—as obligations that must be met in order for us to keep the New Covenant. It is absolutely true that the New Covenant has obligations. But as we have been seeing throughout this book, in the Covenant of Grace (of which the New Covenant is a part) obedience is never the *cause* of covenant blessings. In fact, just the opposite is true. In the New Covenant, the covenant blessings—forgiveness of sin, being declared righteous for Christ's sake, New Life—the covenant blessings are the cause and obedience is the effect.

Of course, most monocovenantalists are not rank legalists. They want to say that the New Covenant is conditioned upon our obedience *and our faith.* If this were true, it would do violence to the biblical doctrine of justification. It would threaten the Gospel because justification would no longer be by grace alone, through faith alone on the basis of Christ's meritorious obedience alone. If our faith and obedience were both conditional[65] obligations of the New Covenant, then our justification would be by God's grace and justice, through our "faith" and works because Christ helped us do it.[66] Thankfully, by His grace alone God justifies the wicked through their faith alone in Christ alone whose merits are imputed to them (Rom. 4:5).

---

[65] In speaking of the Abrahamic covenant, Shepherd says that that covenant was conditional, "but neither were its conditions meritorious," *The Call of Grace: How the Covenant Illuminates Salvation and Evangelism* (Phillipsburg: P&R Publishing, 2000), 22. In his chapter on the New Covenant he says that "the same principles are operative in all the covenants" (p. 49). The logical conclusion, then, is that *all* covenants (including the New Covenant) are conditional, but conditional without merit (whatever that means). Or, to put it another way: if all covenants are made up of promise and obligation, and if the Abrahamic covenant was conditional (without merit), then the New Covenant is also conditional (without merit).

[66] Ibid., 57.

Another way of talking about our obedience is in terms of perseverance. To persevere means to "make it to the end." Again, it is true that the New Testament calls us to persevere until Christ returns (Gal. 6:9; Heb. 2:1-4; 6:4-6; 10:26-31). But does that mean that the outcome of the New Covenant hinges upon our sin-stained works?[67] No. As we have seen time and time again, our works are the *effects* of the New Covenant—Christ's meritorious accomplishments are the *cause*.

If we see someone who claims to be a Christian but lives in unrepentant sin, we can biblically conclude that such a person is not truly a Christian (1 John 3:9). We can conclude this because when God justifies a person, He necessarily begins sanctifying her as well. When we believe, we don't merely receive the justification-benefits of Christ—we receive *all Spiritual blessings* (Eph. 1:3) including sanctification. But that is exactly the opposite of saying that we receive eternal life by "doing the will of God"[68] until Christ comes back. God has (re)created us (in the New Creation) to do good works which He had prepared beforehand for us (Eph. 2:10). God has not only *begun* a good work in us, but He will *complete* that good work as well (Phil. 1:6). If we persevere, it is only because God graciously—in spite of our sin—accomplished our salvation (from beginning to end) in Christ.

So things like obedience and perseverance in the New Covenant turn out to be the *results* of Christ's accomplishment. But since monocovenantalists believe that all covenants are governed by the same principles—promise and obligation—there is no good reason why the Mosaic covenant (or any covenant) should not still

---

[67] Monocovenantalists like Norman Shepherd would say "yes." He plainly states that the way in which we receive what has been promised (eternal life) "is not simply perseverance in *belief*, but perseverance in *doing the will of God*." Ibid., 49. (emphasis his)

[68] Ibid., 49.

be in force. In other words, shouldn't the Mosaic covenant be just as binding on us today as the New Covenant? Norman Shepherd himself puts it best when he asks, "If the new covenant shows the same pattern of promise and obligation as the Mosaic, why was the Mosaic covenant abrogated?"[69]

We have seen the answer to that question in the last two chapters. Israel swore an oath to keep a typological covenant of works. They violated their oath and broke the covenant. That is part of the reason why the Mosaic covenant was abrogated. But the apostle Paul gives us more. The Mosaic covenant ("the Law") functioned as a "pedagogue," a tutor or a schoolmaster in order to drive us to Christ (Gal. 3:24). After all, the Law was added parallel to the Abrahamic covenant in order to *provoke* sin (Gal. 3:19). No one is able to bear that burden (Acts 15:10), and so such a covenant forces its members to cry out, "Who, then, can be saved?" (Mt. 19:25). Again, Paul points us to Christ: the Mosaic covenant was added *until Christ came* (Gal. 3:19). Now that Christ has come, we are no longer under the Law (Gal. 3:25; Rom. 6:1-14). Christ was born under the Law (Gal. 4:4) in order to keep the Law on our behalf (John 17:4-5), and yet also in order to bear the curse of the Law in our place (Gal. 3:13-14). Everything that the Mosaic covenant was about, is complete in Christ. That is why the Mosaic covenant is abrogated.

Of course, the Mosaic covenant was defective because it could not produce heavenly righteousness. The heavenly High Priest came not only to provide the once-for-all-time sacrifice that would cover over the sins of Gods people, but he also provided the heavenly righteousness needed to stand before God. Therefore, it is obsolete.

---

[69] Ibid., 52.

The blood of bulls and goats could not ultimately deal with sin. That truth was built into the animal sacrifices themselves. Imagine being a believing Israelite who wanted to deal with his sin in the way that God had commanded him to deal with it. You would make your way to the temple in Jerusalem where the high priest would sacrifice an animal for the many sins of the covenant community. Though you should have been slain for your sin, the animal seemed to bear your punishment for you. But of course, the animal didn't bear your punishment because the very next year, *another* animal would be slaughtered for *more* of your sins. This process was repeated year after year (Heb. 9:7, 25; 10:1, 3).

The animal sacrifices did not *actually* remove sin, but they pointed to the One who would actually remove sin. Believing Israelites were able to perceive that by faith (Heb. 11). In stark contrast to the high priests of the Old Covenant, our High Priest, Jesus Christ, offered *one* sacrifice that removed all the sins of all of God's people for all time (Heb. 9:25-28). But also in stark contrast to the fallen high priests of the Old Covenant, our High Priest, Jesus Christ was *Himself* the substitutionary sacrifice (Heb. 7:26-28)—the Lamb of God who takes away the sins of the world (Jn. 1:29).

Part of the defectiveness of the Mosaic covenant lay in the fact that its commandments could not impart life.[70] It is true that the Law could not provide *eternal* life (Gal. 2:16). But the Law could provide temporal life because it offered "the good life" in Canaan for Israel's obedience (Lev. 18:5; Gal. 3:12). So even though the difference between the "life" of the Law and the New Life of the New Covenant is as drastic as the difference between the

---

[70] Ibid., 54, 55. Ironically, a few pages later, Shepherd implies that the Law *can* impart life when he says, "Rather, observing the law cannot save a person because the Mosaic system is no longer operative" (p. 56). But what if the Mosaic system *were* still operative? Does Shepherd really mean to say that if the Mosaic system were still operative, then observing the law *could* save a person? That certainly appears to be the implication.

shadow (Canaan) and the reality (Heaven), there was another important difference. In the Mosaic covenant, Israel swore the oath of the covenant. They vowed to be *personally* responsible for keeping the covenant. But as sinners, their oath was as good as broken as they swore it. In total contrast to Israel's oath in the Old Covenant, God swore the oath in the New Covenant. In making Himself personally responsible for keeping the covenant, God's oath was as good as kept (Heb. 6:13-20). Besides His inability to lie, what made God's oath unbreakably sure was the certainty of Christ's—the True Israel's—obedience. By His perfect Law-keeping, His substitutionary death and His victorious resurrection, Jesus became the surety or the guarantor of the New Covenant (Heb. 7:22). Because of Jesus, it is impossible for the New Covenant to be broken and the blessings are absolutely sure.

Because of what Jesus has done, God's covenant has been enlarged to include *all* who trust in Christ—not only believing Jews. The "tent" of God's covenant has been opened wide so that not only the Shemites (believing Jews), but also the Japhethites (believing Gentiles) may dwell there, too (Gen. 9:27 cf. Acts 14:27; 1 Cor. 16:9). He has called us "My people" who were not His people (Hos. 1:8-10; 2:23; Rom. 9:24-33). We Gentiles have been grafted into the one, covenant people of God (Rom. 11:16-24). We Gentiles have come streaming into the New Temple (Is. 60 cf. Mt. 2:1-11; 28:19; Rom. 15:7-13). In fact, Jesus' death has eliminated the division between Jew and Gentile (Eph. 2:11-22) so that in Him there is no longer any distinction between Greek and Jew, between the circumcised and the uncircumcised, barbarian, Scythian, slave and free—instead Christ is all, and Christ is in all (Col. 3:11).

Not only that, but the New Covenant people of God have actually become the New Tabernacle or the New Temple (Amos 9:11-12; Acts 15:13-18). No longer does God make His presence to dwell in a building made with hands. The human body of Jesus Christ is the Temple (Jn. 2:19-22) that has replaced the mere copy that was destroyed in 70 A.D. (Mt. 24:1-2; 24:15-28; Heb. 8:1-6). As we participate in the body and blood of Christ in the Holy Supper, we are formed into the one body of Christ (1 Cor. 10:16-17). So if Christ's body is the New Temple and we are the body of Christ, then we, too, are the New Temple. In fact, the apostles form the foundation of this Temple—Christ Jesus Himself being the corner stone in whom the entire building is joined, growing into a holy temple in the Lord—in whom you are being built together into the dwelling place of God in the Spirit (Eph. 2:20-22 cf. 1 Cor. 3:16).

CONCLUSION

The New Covenant is about what Christ has done for us. He has done nothing less than completely accomplish what the first Adam failed to do. The Last Adam has not only passed His covenantal probation, but He has earned the right to dwell in the Heavenly Kingdom of God. He is the first human being to enter into that ultimate Kingdom. In that sense, He is the firstfruits of the New Humanity—the New Creation people of God (1 Cor. 15:20, 23).

This is why the entire Bible is about Christ from Genesis to Revelation. The first man Adam had all the revelation He needed in the creation around him (including himself as the image of God) and in the specific command God gave him about what not to do ("Do not eat of the tree of the knowledge of good and evil"). All he needed to do was obey as the subordinate king under the Great King. But because he didn't obey, and because he plunged us into a helpless condition of sin, we need another Adam—a New Adam—the Last Adam—to accomplish God's Kingdom-purpose for us.

Because Adam failed, Jesus is the ultimate Seed of the woman who has prevailed—suffering first on the cross, but then entering into His glory (Gen. 3:15). Far better than Noah, Jesus has saved God's entire household because He is the vessel in whom we safely survive God's wrath (1 Pet. 3:20-22). Far better than

Abraham, Jesus Himself is the promise that Abraham only hoped for (Rom. 4; Gal. 3; Heb. 11:8-19). Far better than Isaac, Jesus was the truly righteous man (as well as truly God) who could be not only our human sacrifice, but also our living redeemer (Heb. 11:17-19). Far better than Jacob, Jesus did more than dream about the Heavenly character of the promised land (Gen. 28:10ff.), He ascended into the Heavenly Promised Land (Ps. 110/Mk. 16:19). Far better than Jacob's son Joseph, Jesus has ascended to the right hand—not of Pharaoh, but of God Almighty—and has received that name which is above every name (Phil. 2:9-11). Far better than Moses, Jesus was not just a servant in God's house, but He is the Son over God's house (Heb. 3:1-6). But more than that—though the Law came through Moses, grace and truth have come through Jesus Christ (Jn. 1:17).

He is not only the ultimate Prophet who has come down from Heaven to proclaim that He Himself is the Good News (Acts 3:19-23)—not only the ultimate Priest who has ascended into Heaven itself after offering Himself as the ultimate sacrifice for our sins (Heb. 7:21-28)—not only the ultimate King who now reigns in Heaven at the Father's right hand (Acts 2:29-36)—the Last Adam is also our federal, covenant representative. Whereas Adam's one act of disobedience as our representative earned sin, death and condemnation for us, so the Last Adam's one act of obedience as our representative earned righteousness, life and justification for us (Rom. 5:12-21). This is the clearest evidence for covenant theology: either Adam or Christ is your federal, covenant representative. Though there are some who belong to Christ but are not visibly identified with the true Church—and though there are some unbelievers who are visibly identified with the true Church—if you are under Adam you are condemned, but if you are under Christ you have been declared righteous before God.

Though Adam's covenant violation was imputed to us (Rom. 5:12), our sin and guilt were imputed to Christ on the cross (2 Cor. 5:21). But justification is not merely the absence of guilt.

God has always demanded perfectly righteous obedience. He will accept nothing less. Therefore, in Jesus Christ, the righteousness of God is revealed (Rom. 1:16-17; 3:21-22). But the righteousness that is revealed is not only the righteousness that God demands—it is also God's own righteousness that He has provided on our behalf. Thankfully, He has come to us even in our sin (Rom. 4:5) and credited or imputed to us Christ's perfect obedience as if it were our own (Rom. 3:21-26; ch. 4). So our righteousness does not come from our own obedience to God's Law, but rather from Christ's meritorious obedience (Phil. 3:9; Rom. 3:21-22; 3:28; Gal. 2:16).

In this book, we have seen examples of those who object to the concept of merit altogether. If they are correct, then there is no justification—no Gospel—no Good News. If there were no merit, then it would be impossible for anyone to deserve eternal punishment in Hell (let alone deserve *anything*). There would be no need for the Gospel because there would be nothing that we needed to be saved *from*. More than that, Christ could not have earned anything for us. He could not have pleased God on our behalf by His perfect obedience. Such people have imagined a single covenant with no merit and no federal, covenant representatives. We may call this a "Bible fiction," for the Bible knows of no such covenant.

Instead, what the Bible reveals to us is that the Last Adam came to bear the curse that Adam demerited for us. This ultimate curse was pictured as a shadowy sketch in the Mosaic covenant which thundered: "Cursed is everyone who does not continue to do everything that is written in the Book of the Law" (Deut. 27:26; Gal. 3:10) and "Cursed is everyone who hangs upon a tree" (Deut. 21:23; Gal. 3:13).

The invisible Heavens

Eden

Canaan

Final Judgment for believers

The New Creation

Covenant of Grace

Final Judgment for unbelievers

Covenant of Common Grace

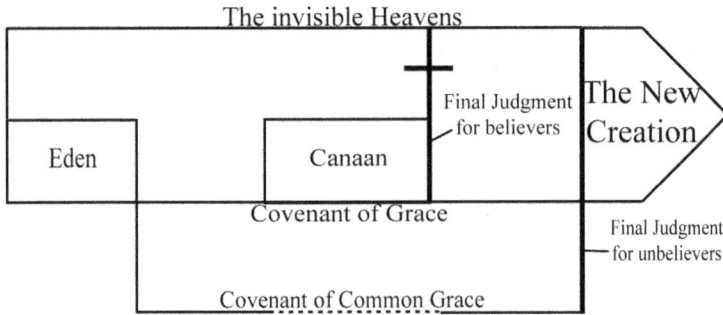

On the cross, Jesus not only brought an end to the Mosaic covenant (though the ultimate judgment spoken of in Lev. 26 and Deut. 28 came when Rome utterly destroyed Jerusalem in 70 A.D.), but as the Last Adam He bore the Final Judgment that we deserved.

But He did not remain in the grave. His obedience to His Father merited eternal life in the New Creation Kingdom *as a human being.* Therefore as the reward for His meritorious, covenantal obedience—and as the first fruits of our own resurrection—God raised His Son by the power of His Holy Spirit.

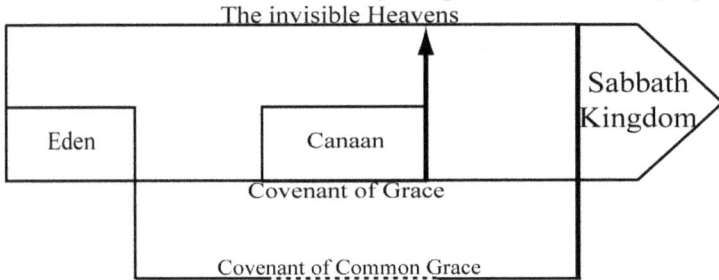

The invisible Heavens

Eden

Canaan

Sabbath Kingdom

Covenant of Grace

Covenant of Common Grace

Now the Last Adam not only lives in an imperishable, glorious, powerful, (Holy) Spiritual, Heavenly body (1 Cor. 15:40-50), but our covenant representative has ascended to sit at the right hand of the Almighty Father. The Last Adam has entered the Sabbath rest of God that Adam only hoped for.

Because He is our representative, and because He has begun the New Creation with His resurrection, we live "between two worlds."

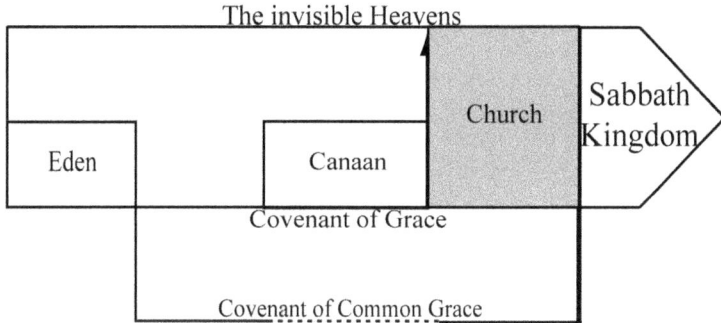

Of course we still live in this world. We are reminded of that every time we get tired, thirsty, hungry, sick or when someone we love dies. But at the same time, we have begun to participate in the world to come (Heaven) *in Christ*. Because He is our covenant representative, Paul is able to say:

> Since then, you have been raised up with Christ, keep seeking the things above where Christ is, seated at the right hand of God. Set your mind upon the things above, not upon the things of the earth. For you have died, and your life is hidden with Christ in God. When Christ who is your life is revealed, then you shall be revealed with Him in glory (Col. 3:1-4).

All of this, and much more, Christ has accomplished for us. Even though our best efforts do not satisfy God's standard of perfection because of the Fall, Christ has kept God's covenant on our behalf. He is the only human being who is inherently pleasing to God. Therefore, God is pleased with us—not because of anything good in us—but because of Christ who was good for us. He has earned all of the New Covenant blessings for us as if we had kept God's original Covenant of Creation perfectly. Our desire to obey God, our attempts at obedience and our New Life are all the blessing-effects of Christ's representative acts on our behalf. Indeed, He became for us wisdom from God, and also righteousness, sanctification and redemption so that just as it is written "Let the one who boasts, boast in the Lord" (1 Cor. 1:30-31).

Appendix 1
We Confess

We Confess

It is very important to remember that we are not the first ones to read the Bible. Many Christians who were far more educated and wise than we, have not only read the Bible, but have collaborated together to summarize what the Bible teaches about essential things. We would do well to do our thinking about the Bible "in dialogue" with the Church that has gone before us. When we forget about or ignore their summaries, we are far more likely to rush headlong into serious error. But we should also be willing to continue to reform our confessions according to God's Word. Below are some of the best confessional statements about covenants and justification. [My comments will be in brackets.]

COVENANT

The Westminster Confession of Faith (1647 - Presbyterian)
Chapter 7: Of God's Covenant with Man

II. The first covenant made with man was a covenant of works,[2] wherein life was promised to Adam; and in him to his posterity,[3] upon condition of perfect and personal obedience.[4]

2. Gen. 2:16-17; Hosea 6:7; Gal. 3:12
3. Gen. 3:22: Rom. 5:12-20; 10:5
4. Gen 2:17; Gal. 3:10

III. Man, by his fall, having made himself incapable of life by that covenant, the Lord was pleased to make a second,[5] commonly called the covenant of grace; wherein he freely offereth unto sinners life and salvation by Jesus Christ; requiring of them faith in him, that they may be saved,[6] and promising to give unto all those that are ordained unto eternal life his Holy Spirit, to make them willing, and able to believe.[7]

5. Gal. 3:21; Rom. 3:20-21; 8:3; Gen. 3:15; see Isa. 42:6
6. John 3:16; Rom. 10:6, 9; Rev. 22:17
7. Acts 13:48; Ezek. 36:26-27; John 6:37, 44-45; I Cor. 12:3

[Notice how the Westminster divines beautifully captured the federal, covenant representation of the two Adams in this section. This document also clearly distinguishes between two different *kinds* of covenants: one based on justice that is conditional for us, called a "covenant of works," and another based on God's grace that is "free" for us called the "covenant of grace." One "mono-covenant" made up of faith-works and grace-justice is completely foreign to the Westminster standards.]

IV. This covenant of grace is frequently set forth in Scripture by the name of a testament, in reference to the death of Jesus Christ the Testator, and to the everlasting inheritance, with all things belonging to it, therein bequeathed.[8]

8. Heb. 9:15-17

Westminster Larger Catechism (1647 - Presbyterian):

Q22: Did all mankind fall in that first transgression ?
A22: The covenant being made with Adam as a public person, not for himself only, but for his posterity, all mankind descending from him by ordinary generation,[1] sinned in him, and fell with him in that first transgression.[2]

1. Acts 17:26
2. Gen. 2:16-17; Rom. 5:12-20; I Cor. 15:21-22

Q30: Doth God leave all mankind to perish in the estate of sin and misery?
A30: God doth not leave all men to perish in the estate of sin and misery,[1] into which they fell by the breach of the first covenant, commonly called the Covenant of Works;[2] but of his mere love and mercy delivereth his elect out of it, and bringeth them into an estate of salvation by the second covenant, commonly called the Covenant of Grace.[3]

1. I Thess. 5:9
2. Gal. 3:10, 12
3. Titus 3:4-7; Gal. 3:21; Rom. 3:20-22

Q32: How is the grace of God manifested in the second covenant?
 A32: The grace of God is manifested in the second covenant, in that he freely provideth and offereth to sinners a Mediator,[1] and life and salvation by him;[2] and requiring faith as the condition to interest them in him, promiseth and giveth his Holy Spirit[3] to all his elect, to work in them that faith,[4] with all other saving graces;[5] and to enable them unto all holy obedience,[5] as the evidence of the truth of their faith[6] and thankfulness to God,[7] and as the way which he hath appointed them to salvation.[8]

1. Gen. 3:15; Isa. 42:6; John 6:27
2. I John 5:11-12
3. John 1:12; 3:16
4. Prov. 1:23
5. II Cor. 4:13
6. Gal. 5:22-23
7. Ezek. 36:27
8. James 2:18, 22
9. II Cor. 5:14-15
10. Eph. 2:18

[Note well that our obedience is the "evidence" of salvation—not part of the way in which we obtain salvation.]

Q35: How is the covenant of grace administered under the New Testament?
 A35: Under the New Testament, when Christ the substance was exhibited, the same covenant of grace was and still is to be administered in the preaching of the word,[1] and the administration of the sacraments of Baptism[2] and the Lord's Supper;[3] in which grace and salvation are held forth in more fulness, evidence, and efficacy, to all nations.[4]

1. Mark 16:15
2. Matt. 28:19-20
3. I Cor. 11:23-25
4. II Cor. 3:6-9; Heb. 8:6, 10-11; Matt. 28:19

Q36: Who is the Mediator of the covenant of grace?
A36: The only Mediator of the covenant of grace is the Lord Jesus Christ,[1] who, being the eternal Son of God, of one substance and equal with the Father,[2] in the fulness of time became man,[3] and so was and continues to be God and man, in two entire distinct natures, and one person, forever.[4]

1. I Tim. 2:5
2. John 1:1, 14; 10:30; Phil. 2:6
3. Gal. 4:4
4. Luke 1:35; Rom. 9:5; Col. 2:9; Heb. 7:24-25

The London Confession of Baptist Faith (1689 - Baptist)
Chapter 7: Of God's Covenant

III. This covenant is revealed in the gospel; first of all to Adam in the promise of salvation by the seed of the woman,[5] and afterwards by farther steps, until the full discovery thereof was completed in the New Testament;[6] and it is founded in that eternal covenant transaction that was between the Father and the Son about the redemption of the elect;[7] and it is alone by the grace of this covenant that all of the posterity of fallen Adam that ever were saved did obtain life and blessed immortality, man being now utterly incapable of acceptance with God upon those terms on which Adam stood in his state of innocency.[8]

5. Gen. 3:15
6. Heb. 1:1
7. II Tim. 1:9; Titus 1:2
8. Heb. 11:6, 13; Rom. 4:1-2; Acts 4:12; John 8:56

[Ironically, the Baptists—who are not known for their covenant theology—have the only confessional statement that teaches the eternal, intratrinitarian Covenant of Redemption.]

JUSTIFICATION

The Augsburg Confession (1530 - Lutheran)
Article 4: Of Justification

Also they teach that men cannot be justified before God by their own strength, merits, or works, but are freely justified for Christ's sake, through faith, when they believe that they are received into favor, and that their sins are forgiven for Christ's sake, who, by His death, has made satisfaction for our sins. This faith God imputes for righteousness in His sight. Rom. 3 and 4.

The Smalcald Articles (1537 - Lutheran)
Article 13: How One is Justified Before God and of Good Works

What I have hitherto and constantly taught concerning this I know not how to change in the least, namely, that by faith, as St. Peter says, we acquire a new and clean heart, and God will and does account us entirely righteous and holy for the sake of Christ, our Mediator. And although sin in the flesh has not yet been altogether removed or become dead, yet He will not punish or remember it.

And such faith, renewal, and forgiveness of sins is followed by good works. And what there is still sinful or imperfect also in them shall not be accounted as sin or defect, even (and that, too) for Christ's sake; but the entire man, both as to his person and his works, is to be called and to be righteous and holy from pure grace and mercy, shed upon us (unfolded) and spread over us in Christ. Therefore we cannot boast of many merits and works, if they are viewed apart from grace and mercy, but as it is written, 1 Cor. 1, 31: He that glorieth, let him glory in the Lord, namely, that he has a gracious

God. For thus all is well. We say, besides, that if good works do not follow, faith is false and not true.

The Genevan Confession (1545 - Continental Reformed)
Article 7: Righteousness in Jesus
Therefore we acknowledge the things which are consequently given to us by God in Jesus Christ: first, that being in our own nature enemies of God and subjects of his wrath and judgment, we are reconciled with him and received again in grace through the intercession of Jesus Christ, so that by his righteousness and guiltlessness we have remission of our sins, and by the shedding of his blood we are cleansed and purified from all our stains.

The Belgic Confession of Faith (1561 - Continental Reformed)
Article 22: Our Justification Through Faith in Jesus Christ
We believe that, to attain the true knowledge of this great mystery, the Holy Spirit kindles in our hearts an upright faith, which embraces Jesus Christ with all His merits, appropriates Him, and seeks nothing more besides Him. For it must needs follow, either that all things which are requisite to our salvation are not in Jesus Christ, or if all things are in Him, that then those who possess Jesus Christ through faith have complete salvation in Him. Therefore, for any to assert that Christ is not sufficient, but that something more is required besides Him, would be too gross a blasphemy; for hence it would follow that Christ was but half a Savior.

Therefore we justly say with Paul, that we *are justified by faith alone*, or *by faith apart from works*. However, to speak more clearly, we do not mean that faith itself justifies us, for it is only an instrument with which we embrace Christ our righteousness. But Jesus Christ, imputing to us all His merits, and so many holy works which He has done for us and in our stead, is our righteousness. And faith is an instrument that keeps us in communion with Him in all His benefits, which, when they become ours, are more than sufficient to acquit us of our sins.

[Here we confess that in justification we embrace Christ "with all His merits."]

Article 23: Wherein Our Justification Before God Consists
We believe that our salvation consists in the remission of our sins for Jesus Christ's sake, and that therein our righteousness before God is implied; as David and Paul teach us, declaring this to be the blessedness of man that *God imputes righteousness to him apart from works.* And the same apostle says that we are *justified freely by his grace, through the redemption that is in Christ Jesus.*

And therefore we always hold fast this foundation, ascribing all the glory to God, humbling ourselves before Him, and acknowledging ourselves to be such as we really are, without presuming to trust in anything in ourselves, or in any merit of ours, relying and resting upon the obedience of Christ crucified alone, which becomes ours when we believe in Him. This is sufficient to cover all our iniquities, and to give us confidence in approaching to God; freeing the conscience of fear, terror, and dread, without following the example of our first father, Adam, who, trembling, attempted to cover himself with fig-leaves. And, verily, if we should appear before God, relying on ourselves or on any other creature, though ever so little, we should, alas! be consumed. And therefore every one must pray with David: *O Jehovah, enter not into judgment with thy servant: for in thy sight no man living is righteous.*

[This article contains echoes of Paul's theology of the two Adams. It is significant that it is an article about justification, because it provides a confessional link for us between covenant and justification.]

The Second Helvetic Confession (1562 - Continental Reformed)
Chapter 15: Of the True Justification of the Faithful

What Is Justification? According to the apostle in his treatment of justification, to justify means to remit sins, to absolve from guilt and punishment, to receive into favor, and to pronounce a man just. For in his epistle to the Romans the apostle says: *It is God who justifies; who is to condemn?* (Rom. 8:33). To justify and to condemn are opposed. And in The Acts of the Apostles the apostle states: *Through Christ forgiveness of sins is proclaimed to you, and by him everyone that believes is freed from everything from which you could not be freed by the law of Moses* (Acts 13:38 f.). For in the Law and also in the Prophets we read: *If there is a dispute between men, and they come into court . . . the judges decide between them, acquitting the innocent and condemning the guilty* (Deut. 25:1). And in Isa., ch. 5: *Woe to those . . . who acquit the guilty for a bribe.*

We Are Justified on Account of Christ. Now it is most certain that all of us are by nature sinners and godless, and before God's judgment-seat are convicted of godlessness and are guilty of death, but that, solely by the grace of Christ and not from any merit of ours or consideration for us, we are justified, that is, absolved from sin and death by God the Judge. For what is clearer than what Paul said: *Since all have sinned and fall short of the glory of God, they are justified by his grace as a gift, through the redemption which is in Christ Jesus* (Rom. 3:23 f.).

Imputed Righteousness. For Christ took upon himself and bore the sins of the world, and satisfied divine justice. Therefore, solely on account of Christ's sufferings and resurrection God is propitious with respect to our sins and does not impute them to us, but imputes Christ's righteousness to us as our own (II Cor. 5:19 ff.; Rom. 4:25), so that now we are not only cleansed and purged from sins or are holy, but also, granted the righteousness of Christ, and so absolved from sin, death and condemnation, are at last righteous and heirs of eternal life. Properly speaking, therefore, God alone justifies us, and justifies only on account of Christ, not imputing sins to us but imputing his righteousness to us.

We Are Justified by Faith Alone. But because we receive this justification, not through any works, but through faith in the mercy of God and in Christ, we therefore teach and believe with the apostle that sinful man is justified by faith alone in Christ, not by the law or any works. For the apostle says: *We hold that a man is justified by faith apart from works of law* (Rom. 3:28). Also: *If Abraham was justified by works, he has something to boast about, but not before God. For what does the scripture say? Abraham believed God, and it was reckoned to him as righteousness. . . . And to one who does not work but believes in him who justified the ungodly, his faith is reckoned as righteousness* (Rom. 4:2 ff.; Gen. 15:6). And again: *By grace you have been saved through faith; and this is not your own doing, it is the gift of God - not because of works, lest any man should boast,* etc. (Eph. 2:8 f.). Therefore, because faith receives Christ our righteousness and attributes everything to the grace of God in Christ, on that account justification is attributed to faith, chiefly because of Christ and not therefore because it is our work. For it is the gift of God.

We Receive Christ By Faith. Moreover, the Lord abundantly shows that we receive Christ by faith, in John, ch. 6, where he puts eating for believing, and believing for eating. For as we receive food by eating, so we participate in Christ by believing. Therefore, we do not share in the benefit of justification partly because of the grace of God or Christ, and partly because of ourselves, our love, works or merit, but we attribute it wholly to the grace of God in Christ through faith. For our love and our works could not please God if performed by unrighteous men. Therefore, it is necessary for us to be righteous before we may love and do good works. We are made truly righteous, as we have said, by faith in Christ purely by the grace of God, who does not impute to us our sins, but the righteousness of Christ, or rather, he imputes faith in Christ to us for righteousness. Moreover, the apostle very clearly derives love from faith when he says: *The aim of our command is love that issues from a pure heart, a good conscience, and a sincere faith* (I Tim. 1:5).

James Compared with Paul. Wherefore, in this matter we are not speaking of a fictitious, empty, lazy and dead faith, but of a living, quickening faith. It is and is called a living faith because it apprehends Christ who is life and makes alive, and shows that it is alive by living works. And so James does not contradict anything in this doctrine of ours. For he speaks of an empty, dead faith of which some boasted but who did not have Christ living in them by faith (James 2:14 ff.). James said that works justify, yet without contradicting the apostle (otherwise he would have to be rejected) but showing that Abraham proved his living and justifying faith by works. This all the pious do, but they trust in Christ alone and not in their own works. For again the apostle said: *It is no longer I who live, but Christ who lives in me; and the life I now live in the flesh I live by faith in the Son of God,*[1] *who loved me and gave himself for me. I do not reject the grace of God; for if justification were through the law, then Christ died to no purpose, etc.* (Gal. 2:20 f.).

1. The Latin reads: "by the faith of the Son of God."

[Note well that faith is living "because it apprehends Christ who is life and makes alive." Faith is *not* living because of good works. Instead, faith "shows that it is alive by living works."]

The Heidelberg Catechism (1563 - Continental Reformed)

Q59: But what does it help you now, that you believe all this?
A59: That I am righteous in Christ before God, and an heir of eternal life.[1]

1. Hab. 2:4; Rom. 1:17; 5:1; 8:16; John 3:36; Titus 3:7

Q60: How are you righteous before God?
A60: Only by true faith in Jesus Christ:[1] that is, although my conscience accuses me, that I have grievously sinned against all the commandments of God, and have never kept any of them,[2] and am still prone always to all evil;[3] yet God, without any merit of mine,[4] of mere grace,[5] grants and imputes to me the perfect satisfaction,[6] righteousness and holiness of Christ,[7] as if I had never committed nor had any sins, and had myself accomplished all the obedience which Christ has fulfilled for me;[8] if only I accept such benefit with a believing heart.[9]

192

1. Rom. 3:21-25; Gal. 2:16; Eph. 2:8-9; Phil. 3:9
2. Rom. 3:9-10
3. Rom. 7:23
4. Titus 3:5
5. Rom. 3:24; Eph. 2:8
6. I John 2:2
7. I John 2:1; Rom. 4:4-5; II Cor. 5:19
8. II Cor. 5:21
9. John 3:18; Rom. 3:28; 10:10

Q61: Why do you say that you are righteous by faith only?
A61: Not that I am acceptable to God on account of the worthiness of my faith, but because only the satisfaction, righteousness and holiness of Christ is my righteousness before God;[1] and I can receive the same and make it my own in no other way than by faith only.[2]

1. I Cor. 1:30; 2:2
2. I John 5:10; Isa. 53:5; Gal. 3:22; Rom. 4:16

The French Confession (1571 - Continental Reformed)
Article 17:

We believe that by the perfect sacrifice that the Lord Jesus offered on the cross,[1] we are reconciled to God, and justified before; for we can not be acceptable to him, nor become partakers of the grace of adoption, except as he pardons (all) our sins, and blots them out.[2] Thus we declare that through Jesus Christ we are cleansed and made perfect; by his death we are fully justified, and through him only can we be delivered from our iniquities and transgressions.[3]

1. II Cor. 5:19; Heb. 5:7-9
2. I Peter 2:24-25
3. Heb. 9:14; Eph. 5:26; I Peter 1:18-19

Article 18:
We believe that all our justification rests upon the remission of our sins, in which also is our only blessedness, as says David (Psa. 32:2).[1] We therefore reject all other means of justification before God,[2] and without claiming any virtue or merit, we rest simply in the obedience of Jesus Christ, which is imputed to us as much to blot out all our sins as to make us find grace and favor in the sight of God. And, in fact, we believe that in falling away from this foundation, however slightly, we could not find rest elsewhere, but should always be troubled. For as much as we are never at peace with God till we resolve to be loved in Jesus Christ, for of ourselves we are worthy of hatred.

1. John 17:23; Rom. 4:7-8; 8:1-3; II Cor. 5:19-20
2. I Tim. 2:5; I John 2:1; Rom. 5:19; Acts 4:12

The Thirty-Nine Articles of Religion (1571 - Anglican/Church of England)

Article 11: Of the Justification of Man

We are accounted righteous before God, only for the merit of our Lord and Saviour Jesus Christ by Faith, and not for our own works or deservings. Wherefore, that we are justified by Faith only, is a most wholesome Doctrine, and very full of comfort, as more largely expressed in the Homily of Justification.

Article 12: Of Good Works

Albeit that Good Works, which are the fruits of Faith, and follow after Justification, cannot put away our sins, and endure the severity of God's judgment; yet are they pleasing and acceptable to God in Christ, and do spring out necessarily of a true and lively Faith; insomuch that by them a lively Faith may be as evidently known as a tree discerned by the fruit.

[The Anglicans rightly confess that good works are the "fruits" or *effects* of faith—that good works *"follow after* Justification," not come before as part of the cause. Our "good" works cannot "endure the severity of God's judgment; yet are they pleasing and acceptable to God *in Christ...*"]

Article 13: Of Works Before Justification

Works done before the grace of Christ, and the Inspiration of the Spirit, are not pleasant to God, forasmuch as they spring not of faith in Jesus Christ; neither do they make men meet to receive grace, or (as the School-authors say) deserve grace of congruity: yea rather, for that they are not done as God hath willed and commanded them to be done, we doubt not but they have the nature of sin.

The Westminster Confession of Faith (1647 - Presbyterian)

Chapter 11: Of Justification

I. Those whom God effectually calleth, he also freely justifieth:[1] not by infusing righteousness into them, but by pardoning their sins, and by accounting and accepting their persons as righteous; not for anything wrought in them, or done by them, but for Christ's sake alone; nor by imputing faith itself, the act of believing, or any other evangelical obedience to them, as their righteousness; but by imputing the obedience and satisfaction of Christ unto them,[2] they receiving and resting on him and his righteousness, by faith; which faith they have not of themselves, it is the gift of God.[3]

1. Rom. 3:24; 5:15-16; 8:30
2. Rom. 3:22-28; 4:5-8; 5:17-19; II Cor. 5:19, 21; Titus 3:5, 7; Eph. 1:7; Jer. 23:6; I Cor. 1:30-31
3. John 1:12; 6:44-45, 65; Acts 10:43; 13:38-39; Phil. 1:29; 3:9; Eph. 2:7-8

II. Faith, thus receiving and resting on Christ and his righteousness, is the alone instrument of justification:[4] yet is it not alone in the person justified, but is ever accompanied with all other saving graces, and is no dead faith, but worketh by love.[5]

4. John 3:18, 36; Rom. 3:28; 5:1
5. James 2:17, 22, 26; Gal. 5:6

III. Christ, by his obedience and death, did fully discharge the debt of all those that are thus justified, and did make a proper, real, and full satisfaction to his Father's justice in their behalf.[6] Yet, inasmuch as he was given by the Father for them;[7] and his obedience and satisfaction accepted in their stead;[8] and both, freely, not for anything in them; their justification is only of free grace;[9] that both the exact justice and rich grace of God might be glorified in the justification of sinners.[10]

6. Mark 10:45; Rom. 5:8-10, 18-19; Gal. 3:13; I Tim. 2:5-6; Heb. 1:3; 10:10, 14; Dan. 9:24, 26; see Isa. 52:13-53:12
7. Rom. 8:32; John 3:16
8. II Cor. 5:21; Eph. 5:2; Phil. 2:6-9; Isa. 53:10-11
9. Rom. 3:24; Eph. 1:7
10. Rom. 3:26; Eph. 2:7; Zech. 9:9; Isa. 45:21

IV. God did, from all eternity, decree to justify all the elect,[11] and Christ did, in the fullness of time, die for their sins, and rise again for their justification:[12] nevertheless, they are not justified, until the Holy Spirit doth, in due time, actually apply Christ unto them.[13]
11. Rom. 8:29, 30; Gal. 3:8; I Peter 1:2, 19-20
12. Gal. 4:4; I Tim. 2:6; Rom. 4:25
13. Eph. 2:3; Titus 3:3-7; Gal. 2:16; cf. Col. 1:21-22

VI. The justification of believers under the old testament was, in all these respects, one and the same with the justification of believers under the new testament.[17]

17. Gal. 3:9, 13-14; Rom. 4:6-8, 22-24; 10:6-13; Heb. 13:8

The Westminster Larger Catechism (1647 - Presbyterian):

Q69: What is the communion in grace which the members of the invisible church have with Christ?
A69: The communion in grace which the members of the invisible church have with Christ, is their partaking of the virtue of his mediation, in their justification,[1] adoption,[2] sanctification, and whatever else, in this life, manifests their union with him.[3]

1. Rom. 8:30
2. Eph. 1:5
3. I Cor. 1:30

Q70: What is justification?
A70: Justification is an act of God's free grace unto sinners,[1] in which he pardoneth all their sins, accepteth and accounteth their persons righteous in his sight;[2] not for any thing wrought in them, or done by them,[3] but only for the perfect obedience and full satisfaction of Christ, by God imputed to them,[4] and received by faith alone.[5]

1. Rom. 3:22, 24-25; 4:5
2. II Cor. 5:19, 21; Rom. 3:22-25, 27-28
3. Titus 3:5, 7; Eph. 1:7
4. Rom. 4:6-8; 5:17-19
5. Acts 10:43; Gal. 2:16; Phil. 3:9

[It is not because our faith is "living and active" that we are justified, but "only for the perfect obedience and full satisfaction of Christ, by God imputed to (us) and received by faith alone."]

Q71: How is justification an act of God's free grace?
A71: Although Christ, by his obedience and death, did make a proper, real, and full satisfaction to God's justice in the behalf of

them that are justified;[1] yet inasmuch as God accepteth the satisfaction from a surety, which he might have demanded of them, and did provide this surety, his own only Son,[2] imputing his righteousness to them,[3] and requiring nothing of them for their justification but faith,[4] which also is his gift,[5] their justification is to them of free grace.[6]

1. Rom. 5:8-10, 19
2. II Tim. 2:5-6; Heb. 7:22; 10:10; Matt. 20:28; Dan. 9:24, 26; Isa. 53:4-6, 10-12; Rom. 8:32; I Peter 1:18-19
3. II Cor. 5:21
4. Rom. 3:24-25
5. Eph. 2:8
6. Eph. 1:7

Q72: What is justifying faith?
A72: Justifying faith is a saving grace,[1] wrought in the heart of a sinner by the Spirit [2] and word of God,[3] whereby he, being convinced of his sin and misery, and of the disability in himself and all other creatures to recover him out of his lost condition,[4] not only assenteth to the truth of the promise of the gospel,[5] but receiveth and resteth upon Christ and his righteousness, therein held forth, for pardon of sin,[6] and for the accepting and accounting of his person righteous in the sight of God for salvation.[7]

1. Heb. 10:39
2. II Cor. 4:13; Eph. 1:17-19
3. Rom. 10:14, 17
4. Acts 2:37; 4:12; 16:30; John 16:8-9; Rom. 5:6; Eph. 2:1
5. Eph. 1:13
6. John 1:12; Acts 10:43; 16:31
7. Phil. 3:9; Acts 15:11

Q73: How doth faith justify a sinner in the sight of God?
A73: Faith justifies a sinner in the sight of God, not because of those other graces which do always accompany it, or of good works that are the fruits of it,[3] nor as if the grace of faith, or any act thereof, were imputed to him for his justification;[2] but only as it is an instrument by which he receiveth and applies Christ and his righteousness.[3]

1. Gal. 3:11; Rom. 3:28
2. Rom. 4:5; 10:10
3. John 1:12; Phil. 3:9; Gal. 2:16

[Here we confess that it is not our faith (and certainly not our "faithful obedience") that is imputed or credited as righteousness, it is Christ and *His* righteousness that is imputed to us. We receive His righteousness and obedience as our own by faith alone.]

The Waldensian Confession (1655 - Continental Reformed)

Article 14:
That God so loved the world, that is to say, those whom he has chosen out of the world, that he gave his own Son to save us by his most perfect obedience (especially that obedience which he manifested in suffering the cursed death of the cross), and also by his victory over the devil, sin, and death.

Article 16:
That the Lord Jesus having fully reconciled us unto God, through the blood of his cross, it is by virtue of his merits only, and not of our works, that we are absolved and justified in his sight.

Article 18:
That this faith is the gracious and efficacious work of the Holy Spirit, who enlightens our souls, and persuades them to lean and rest upon the mercy of God, and so to apply the merits of Jesus Christ.

Article 19:

That Jesus Christ is our true and only Mediator, not only redeeming us, but also interceding for us, and that by virtue of his merits and intercession we have access unto the Father, to make our supplications unto him, with a holy confidence that he will grant our requests, it being needless to have recourse to any other intercessor besides himself.

Appendix 2
Glossary

Glossary

Antithesis/Antithetical: opposite. For example, faith is the antithesis of unbelief, justice/works is antithetical to grace/faith, obedience is the antithesis of disobedience, etc.

Common Grace: the general kindness that God shows to all humanity (believers and unbelievers) in spite of our sin and the eternal punishment we deserve. It is not saving grace, and it does not give unbelievers any help toward faith or God-pleasing obedience. Common grace simply provides a stable environment for humanity so that the second person of the Trinity could become incarnate in history for the salvation of God's people.

Consummation: God's bringing to completion, the final and ultimate stage of the Kingdom of God–the arrival of the New Heavens and the New Earth.

Covenant: an *oath-sworn, legally binding relationship, enforced by God*. A covenant can be identified as one of "works" or one of "grace" based upon which party does the oath-swearing. When man swears the oath, it is a Covenant of Works. When God swears the oath, it is a Covenant of Grace.

Culture: every part of life *outside of* the Church. That is, anything other than the Church's God-ordained activities (e.g., preaching, right administration of the sacraments, prayer, evangelism, etc.).

Demerit: the opposite of merit (see definition of Merit below). Demerit is *anything less than* the perfect fulfillment of the requirements/commands that God demands in His covenant.

Elect: that group of people, *chosen* by God from "before the foundations of the world," to enjoy eternal life with Him in His heavenly Kingdom, in spite of the Fall.

Eschatology: From the Greek word *eschatos*, meaning "end," "final," maybe even "ultimate" or "goal." But it should not be thought of exclusively in terms of "future things," or "the end times." There are four important senses involved in this term: 1) The *eternal reality* of the Kingdom Paradise which God promised to Adam in the Covenant of Works, 2) The *immutable* or *unchangeable state* of perfect life in the presence of God, 3) the *heavenly goal* of the promised Kingdom under the Covenant of Works, 4) The *final stage* of the Kingdom of God.

Faith: looking away from anything in or about ourselves to Christ. Faith is not praiseworthy in and of itself. It is simply an *instrument* by which we accept, receive and rest upon Christ alone. Historically, Protestants have distinguished between three different biblical uses of the word "faith": *notitia* (Latin, meaning *knowledge*), *ascensus* (Latin, meaning approval), *fiducia* (Latin, meaning *confidence, trust, assurance*). It is this last term—fiducia—that is the most important sense of "faith" for salvation.

Faithfulness: Though it has the root word "faith," the word *faithfulness* actually refers to action—even *obedient* action. Webster's Dictionary even uses such phrases as "firmly adhering to duty," and "constant in performance of duties or services" to define *faithfulness*. It is true that the Bible calls us to be faithful servants of Christ. But we are not saved by *our* faithfulness to God. We are saved by *God's* faithfulness to us in the person and work of Christ.

Grace: the demerited favor of God—or, God's favor toward us *in spite of* Adam's guilt imputed to us, our own sin and the punishment we deserve as a result. See Romans 4:4-5.

Justice: the principle of fairness in reward and punishment. The principle of justice ensures that "we get what we deserve." Justice is about what we deserve, and so justice is also about merit.

Legalism: denies that Christ's work is enough, by requiring that we do something personally and individually to please God. Do not be fooled: preachers and teachers do not have to explicitly say "Christ's work is not enough" in order to be engaged in legalism. Legalism simply involves ignoring Christ's role as the Last Adam, our covenant representative. Therefore, any teaching that implies that we can sufficiently please God by our faithful obedience automatically turns into legalism because it imagines that we can please God apart from or without the meritorious obedience of Christ on our behalf.

Merit: the acts or duties that *perfectly* *fulfill* the requirements/commands that God demands *in His covenant*. God's interpretations and definitions are the only ones that count. Apart from God's covenants, merit has no meaning.

Moralism: bare, abstract ethical prescriptions without any consideration or understanding about what Christ has done for us. It is morals for morals' sake alone. Moralism is a preoccupation with our obedience to the exclusion of Christ's meritorious obedience imputed to us. Simply ignoring the sufficiency of Christ's work or impatiently wanting to "get beyond" Christ's work to the "really important stuff" of our practical, daily lives automatically turns any teaching about our obedience into moralism. This does not mean that the category of ethics is inherently unbiblical. Quite to the contrary, it means that always and everywhere, God's commands to us are rooted in, and flow out of God's mighty acts/deeds in real, time-space history. The events of God's works in history come before His commands and therefore constrain us to obey. (e.g., "For if we have become united with him in the likeness of his death, certainly we shall also be in the likeness of his resurrection; knowing this, that our old self was crucified with him, that our body of sin might be done away with, so that we would no longer be slaves to sin... Therefore do not let sin reign in your mortal body, so that you obey its lusts." Rom. 6:1-14, NASB)

Pre-redemptive: literally "before redemption." Redemption began *after* and *as a result of* the Fall. So the term "pre-redemptive" refers to the period of history *before the Fall*.

Probation: a period of testing based upon one's active and passive obedience, the outcome of which is a reward for obedience or punishment for disobedience. This is the situation that God placed Adam into at his creation (Gen. 1:26-28; 2:17) and the situation that God placed Christ, the Second Adam into at his incarnation (John 17:4-5). Adam failed his probation for us; Christ passed his probation for us.

Redemption/Redemptive: to buy back, to pay a ransom price for someone. As a result of the Fall, we are all in bondage to sin. Christ released us from that bondage by the price He paid on the cross. In other words, He redeemed us. The term "redemptive" is an adjective that describes other nouns. In this book, part of the covenant history we have explored was *redemptive* history—that period of time from the Fall to the Consummation. But what makes that history *redemptive* is God's actions and revelation leading up to the life, death, resurrection and ascension of Christ. That history is *redemptive* because it is all about the price Christ would pay and has paid to free God's people from the curse of the Fall.

Sanctions: the *consequences* or *outcomes* of a covenant that are *enforced by God*.

Theocracy: God's holy reign (Kingship) and realm (Kingdom) that *He* establishes. A theocracy is visible and external (though Christ's current theocracy is temporarily hidden until His second arrival). In a theocracy, everything is holy—set apart and consecrated to God (i.e., the opposite of common).

Type/Typology/Typological: From the Greek word *tupos* (Rom. 5:14c), a type is an earthly picture of a heavenly or future reality. Thus, typology would be the study of those Old Testament people, objects and events which pictured the Kingdom-earning work of the person of Christ. The New Testament gives us warrant to identify and study these "types" in passages like (Rom. 5:12-18/1 Cor. 15:45; 1 Cor. 10:1-4; Heb. 3:1-6; 11:14-16, etc. The important point, however, is that Christ is the ultimate *anti-type* or fulfillment of all types. Everything in Scripture finds its fulfillment in Him and His work. Thus, when the sun rises, the shadows (types) go away (cf, Col. 2:17).

Glossary

Appendix 3
Recommended Reading

Recommended Reading

Baldwin, William.
> Bettercovenant.org (Rev. Baldwin has many helpful essays on covenant theology, justification and the implications of both for the Christian life.)

Bierma, Lyle D. *German Calvinism in the Confessional Age: The Covenant Theology of Caspar Olevianus.* (Olevianus was one of the earliest Reformed theologians to develop covenant theology.)

Calvin, John. *Institutes of the Christian Religion.* (Calvin's development of the Law-Gospel contrast is done in covenantal terms.)

Clark, R. Scott, ed. *Covenant, Justification and Pastoral Ministry: Essays by the Faculty of Westminster Seminary California.* (Advanced reading.)

Horton, Michael. *God of Promise: Introducing Covenant Theology.* (In this beginning level book, Dr. Horton treats aspects of covenant theology outside the scope of this book: ancient near eastern treaties, the sacraments of the Old and New Covenants, etc.)

Irons, Lee. "Redefining Merit: An Examination of Medieval Presuppositions in Covenant Theology" in *Creator, Redeemer, Consummator: A Festschrift for Meredith G. Kline.* (This is a helpful essay on merit at an advanced level.)

—. www.upper-register.com (Lee Irons has many helpful essays on covenant theology as it relates to other areas of theology.)

Jeon, Jeong Koo. *Covenant Theology: John Murray's and Meredith G. Kline's Response to the Historical Development of Federal Theology in Reformed Thought.*

—. *Covenant Theology and Justification by Faith: The Shepherd Controversy and Its Impacts.*

Karlberg, Mark W. *Covenant Theology in Reformed Perspective: Collected Essays and Book Reviews in Historical, Biblical, and Systematic Theology.* (Dr. Karlberg does an outstanding job of showing that the covenant theology contained in this book, especially as it deals with the Mosaic Covenant, has been the classic, Reformed view from the beginning.)

—. *Federalism and the Westminster Tradition: Reformed Orthodoxy at the Crossroads.*

—. *Gospel Grace: The Modern-Day Controversy.*

Kline, Meredith G. *By Oath Consigned: A Reinterpretation of the Covenant Signs of Circumcision and Baptism.* (Although by the end of his life, Dr. Kline preferred not to have people read this book due to developments within his own theology, it remains a helpful analysis of circumcision and baptism as signs and seals of divine covenants. For a helpful analysis of corrections Dr. Kline *might* have made, see http://www.upper-register.com/blog/?cat=26 by one of his brightest students, Lee Irons.)

—. "Covenant Theology Under Attack" (unpublished paper, available at http://www.upper-register.com/papers/ct_under_attack.html)

—. *Glory in our Midst: A Biblical-Theological Reading of Zechariah's Night Visions.*

—. *God, Heaven and Har Magedon: A Covenantal Tale of Cosmos and Telos.*

—. *Images of the Spirit.* (This is particularly helpful for understanding the prophets and the New Covenant.)

—. *Kingdom Prologue: Genesis Foundations for a Covenantal Worldview.* (This is Dr. Kline's *magnum opus.* It treats in great detail what we have only been able to treat briefly in this book.)

—. *The Structure of Biblical Authority.* (In this book, Dr. Kline connects biblical covenants with the canon of Scripture. Be sure to read about Intrusion Ethics.)

Lillback, Peter A. *The Binding of God: Calvin's Role in the Development of Covenant Theology.* (Part One of this book is most helpful in establishing the legitimate contribution of John Calvin to the development of Reformed covenant theology. However, I do **not** endorse the theological conclusions drawn in Part Two.)

Modern Reformation Magazine at http://www.modernreformation.org/ (Good, entry-level reading)

Olevianus, Caspar. *A Firm Foundation: An Aid to Interpreting the Heidelberg Catechism.*

Reformation Ink: the largest collection of Reformation primary source material http://homepage.mac.com/shanerosenthal/reformationink /index.html

Tipton, Lane G. http://www.two-age.org/online_sermons.htm#LTipton (Dr. Tipton is masterful in his clear presentation of covenant theology for the uninitiated.)

Recommended Reading

Vos, Geerhardus. *Biblical Theology*. (Dr. Vos was the forerunner of
    Dr. Kline. This book is particularly insightful.)

—. *Redemptive History and Biblical Interpretation: The Shorter Writings of
    Geerhardus Vos*. Ed. Richard B. Gaffin. (Among many other
    helpful essays, Dr. Vos has a valuable analysis of the history
    of Reformed covenant theology in this volume.)

—. *The Eschatology of the Old Testament*. Ed. James T. Dennison Jr.

—. *The Pauline Eschatology*.

—. *The Teaching of the Epistle to the Hebrews*. (As Dr. Vos says,
    Hebrews is "the Epistle of the [covenant]." His insights here
    simply must not be missed.)

Waters, Guy Prentiss. *The Federal Vision and Covenant Theology: A
    Comparative Analysis*. (The Federal Vision advocates a
    covenant theology that confuses justice and grace as well as
    justification and sanctification. Dr. Waters provides a
    helpful analysis.)

—. *Justification and the New Perspectives on Paul: A Review and
    Response*. (The New Perspectives on Paul also advocate a
    covenant theology that confuses justice and grace,
    justification and sanctification. Dr. Waters' analysis is
    helpful.)

Witsius, Herman. *The Economy of the Covenants Between God and
    Man: Comprehending A Complete Body of Divinity*. (Writing in
    the 1600s, Witsius clearly develops the eschatological nature
    of the covenant of works and anticipates Meredith Kline in
    some significant ways with regard to the Mosaic Covenant.)

Index of Scripture

Index of Scripture

www.ingramcontent.com/pod-product-compliance
Lightning Source LLC
Chambersburg PA
CBHW060920040426

42445CB00011B/706

9 780615 241401